A Guide to
Post-Keynesian
Economics

A Guide to
Post-Keynesian
Economics

EDITED BY ALFRED S. EICHNER
WITH A FOREWORD BY JOAN ROBINSON

M. E. Sharpe, Inc.
White Plains, New York

Second printing

Copyright © 1978, 1979 by M. E. Sharpe, Inc.

All rights reserved. No part of this book may be reproduced in any
form without written permission from the publisher.

Design: Laurence Lustig

Library of Congress Catalog Card Number: 79-1971

Publisher's International Standard Book Number: 0-87332-142-1 (hardcover)
0-87332-146-4 (paperback)

Distributor's International Standard Book Number: 0-394-50758-4 (hardcover)
0-394-73726-1 (paperback)

Distributed by Pantheon Books, a division of Random House, Inc.

Printed in the United States of America

Contents

Preface

Late in the day, after they have had two or three drinks, many economics professors will begin to admit to their own reservations about the theory which forms the core of the economics curriculum. The theory, they will acknowledge, is at odds with much that is known about the behavior of economic institutions. "But what else is there to teach our students?" they will ask.

This question, it turns out, can readily be answered. There does exist an alternative to the "neoclassical synthesis" presented to students in introductory, intermediate, and advanced economics courses. The alternative is the post-Keynesian theory which is the subject of this book.

And yet few professors of economics seem aware of this alternative—and fewer still seem willing to expose their students to it. Could this be because they are not sufficiently familiar with post-Keynesian theory—this despite the fact that the main ideas are now more than twenty years old? While an article outlining the major points of difference between the prevailing neoclassical theory and the post-Keynesian alternative appeared in the *Journal of Economic Literature* only a few years back (Eichner and Kregel, 1975), could it be that the article was pitched at too high a technical level? Was the article perhaps too brief to bring out all the important areas of economics touched on by the new approach? Indeed, was it still possible for open-minded colleagues not to appreciate how fundamental was the challenge of post-Keynesian theory to economic orthodoxy? A consideration of this set of possibilities made it evident that there was a need for a series of articles on post-Keynesian theory, written for the neophyte in economics. Whatever reason economics professors may have for not exposing their students to post-Keynesian theory, it should not be because the theory is inaccessible either to them or to their students.

Fortunately, I had already been approached by Mike Sharpe, the editor of *Challenge*, about a follow-up to my book *The Megacorp and Oligopoly* for his magazine. The best follow-up, I told him, would be a series of articles on post-Keynesian theory, since the book was only a part of that much larger literature. He readily agreed to this suggestion, and that was the beginning of the collaboration which produced, first, the series of articles in *Challenge* and now, their appearance here in book form with an introduction by Joan Robinson.

The collaboration has been a happy one for several reasons. First there is the sympathy with which not only Mike but indeed all the staff of *Challenge* and M. E. Sharpe, Inc. has approached the project. It is hard to imagine how they could have been more supportive. Second there has been the insistence by Mike that the articles, here transformed into book chapters, be intelligible even to those without special training in economics. This insistence has served as an important check on the ideas being presented—a check generally absent in scholarly journals. The actual task of carrying out this mandate has fallen, first, on Murray Yanowitch, the managing editor of *Challenge*, and then, secondarily, on Mike and Jackie Sharpe. The clarity of expression and coherence of ideas is due largely to their extraordinary editing efforts. Acknowledgement needs also to be made of Arnold Tovell's decisive role in shepherding the book through to publication once the articles had appeared in *Challenge*.

The individuals most responsible for the appearance of this book are, however, the authors of the individual essays. They have each made a special contribution to the better understanding of post-Keynesian theory. In some cases, they have extended the approach to areas of economics not generally associated with post-Keynesian theory, and in most cases they have actually added to the articulation of a distinctly post-Keynesian paradigm in economics. It is to them that the primary credit for the book belongs. I am particularly grateful to the contributors who have taken on areas of economics outside their primary fields of interest. All of them, however, through their competence and cooperation, have made my job as editor a relatively easy one. And the same is true, of course, of the staff at M. E. Sharpe, Inc.

Alfred S. Eichner
May 1979

JOAN ROBINSON

Foreword

When Keynes was writing *The General Theory*, his main difference from the school from which he was struggling to escape lay in the recognition of the problem of effective demand, which they ignored. It was for this reason that he put everyone from Ricardo to Pigou into one category, and for this reason that he overvalued Malthus. After the book was published, he drew the line differently. He saw that the main distinction was that he recognized, and they ignored, the obvious fact that expectations of the future are necessarily uncertain.

It is from this point that post-Keynesian theory takes off. The recognition of uncertainty undermines the traditional concept of equilibrium.

I

Any economic action, even buying a bus ticket, is directed to its future consequences; the decisions or choices that led to the action have been determined either by mere convention or by expectations about the outcome. The fact that the future cannot be known for certain when choices are being made implies that the concept of microeconomic equilibrium in a competitive market is self-contradictory. When a market is in equilibrium, all participants are satisfied that, in the circumstances in which they were placed, they made the best possible choices, but they could not have done so unless they knew, when choices were open, what the outcome was going to be. Equilibrium is conceivable only in a completely traditional economy, where everyone knows what everyone else will do. But in that situation, there are no decisions to be taken or choices to be made.

In a competitive market, as it is usually described, choices concerned with offers and demands appear to be made simultaneously. This means that such a market can apply only to exchanges of ready-made goods, as in the famous case of prisoners of war exchanging the contents of their Red Cross parcels. Where supply involves production, decisions involving offers have to be made in advance before buyers can exercise their choices.

The slogan that the free play of market forces allocates scarce resources between alternative uses is incomprehensible. At any moment the stocks of means of production in existence are more or less specific. The level of output may be higher or lower with the state of demand but there is very little play in the composition of output. Changes in the adaptation of resources to demand can come about only through the process of investment; but plans for investment are made in the light of expectations about the future which are rarely perfectly fulfilled, and therefore have to be drawn up with a wide margin of error.

Keynes confined his argument almost entirely to the short-period aspect of investment, that is, as a booster to effective demand. He paid little attention to the long-period aspect of investment, that is, its capacity to increase the stock of means of production. (He did discuss a process of long-run accumulation in Chapter 17 of *The General Theory* but it is not at all easy to make this consistent with the rest of the book.) It was left for post-Keynesian critics to tackle the neoclassical notion of the choice of technique for the production of salable commodities based on "rational substitution among resource inputs . . . as their relative prices change." (See the essay by Richard X. Chase, page 74.) Here, it was only necessary to ask the question: *When* do prices change? Investment in long-lived plant is planned in the light of expectations held when the plans are drawn up. During the working lifetime of the plant, prices and many other circumstances—in particular the state of technical development—will change and plans for the next lot of plant to be created will generally be different.

II

Piero Sraffa attacked the notion of "factor prices" from quite a different angle. He set up a model of a technique for producing a particular flow of output with a given labor force, requiring a particular flow of inputs. This can be specified in physical terms. When the system is in a self-reproducing state —inputs being replaced as they are used up—there is a flow of net output also specified in physical terms. Here technology does not determine distribution, through "marginal productivity" or in any other way. Nor do "factor prices" influence technology. Ricardo postulated that the real-wage rate is given in physical terms, being governed by the customary standard of life of the workers. Then, as Sraffa shows, all prices, the value of the stock of capital, and the rate of profit are determined. But Sraffa widened the analysis by allowing the real wage to be a proportion of net output. Then corresponding to each share of wages, there is a share of profits in net output, a rate of profit on capital, and a set of prices for all inputs and outputs, in any numeraire or unit of account.

Sraffa took a great deal of trouble to construct an unexceptionable numeraire—the standard commodity—but once we have understood the argument we can interpret it in terms of the Keynesian wage unit. Taking as numeraire the average money wage of a unit of labor time, we see that a higher level of money prices indicates a higher rate of profit and a lower real wage.

All this was fully worked out in terms of a one-technique system, in which all inputs used up in the process of production are replaced in kind, which entails the assumption that the same technique is going to continue to be used. Then Sraffa introduced technical change in a manner which unfortunately confused the issue.

Into the specification of the model he introduced an alternative method of production, that is, a difference in the combination of inputs required, for one of the outputs. This does not represent an event, a new discovery made at a particular date in history. It is merely the economist manipulating his assumptions to illustrate a point. Nor is it an absolute improvement in technology in the sense that the second method is preferable to the first at any wage rate, and drives it out of existence. At some levels of real wages the second method yields a higher rate of profit; at others, the first. When the two techniques are compared, it is seen that the one which is eligible at the lower rate of profit does not necessarily require "more capital," that is, a higher value of the stock of means of production with the same amount of labor employed. Furthermore it is seen that one technique may be eligible at widely different rates of profit, while the other is eligible at rates in between.

The tremendous furore that arose over "reswitching" (see the essay by Richard X. Chase, page 72) did not help to dispose of the neoclassical production function but rather gave it a second lease of life, because of all the subtleties that could be introduced into the discussion of pseudo-production functions, representing alternative techniques all coexisting at the same date. (A pseudo-production function is a supposed mathematical relationship between labor and "capital-inputs," and the output of goods and services. See the essay by Jan Kregel.)

The participants in the controversy, on both sides, failed to observe that it had nothing whatever to do with the analysis of the choice of technique or the determination of the rate of profit in a process of accumulation going on through historical time.

Perhaps I am partly to blame for introducing the expression "a book of blueprints" for an imaginary list of mutually non-superior techniques all available at once, but at least I did insist that my pseudo-production function could be used only for comparing stocks of capital each already in existence.

III

Professor Samuelson devised a particular form of the pseudo-production function. He assumed that there were a number of techniques for producing an output of a homogeneous commodity, each using a different type of "machine." For each technique, the ratio of "machines" to labor was the same for producing "machines" and for producing the commodity. Thus he postulated within each technique a uniform capital-to-labor ratio or, in Marxian terms, organic composition of capital. Then, labor-value prices ruled. For each technique, the value of the stock of machines in terms of the commodity was then independent of the rate of profit. There was no scope for reversals and reswitching. When the techniques are arranged in descending order of output per unit of labor, they are in ascending order of the rate of profit. Their profile is then exactly like that of a "well-behaved production function." This attempt to rationalize the neoclassical theory in fact makes it all the easier to see where the basic fallacies lie.

In this picture, the technique with the highest output per man employed requires the highest value of capital per man. In neoclassical philosophy, the higher output is due to the greater quantity of capital. Capital is regarded as "a factor of production" which has its own "marginal productivity."

This is an ancient misconception. Differences in productivity arise from differences in technology—in the manner of
making use of human capacities and the qualities of inputs,
and in the manner of utilizing energy. The transition from a
less to a more productive technique *may* require a higher
ratio of the value of capital per man employed but it is by no
means necessary that this should be the case. Innovations
may have a capital-saving as well as a capital-using bias. The
"stylized facts" of industrial growth with a constant rate of
profit and a constant capital-to-output ratio are realized
when technical change is neutral and real wages rise at the
same pace as output per unit of labor. Accumulation and
technical change must be seen as going forward through time,
not as climbing up a pre-existing schedule of known techniques.

The second great fallacy in Professor Samuelson's conception of accumulation is that it begins where output, with a
given labor force, is lowest and the rate of profit highest,
while accumulation is supposed gradually to raise the capital-
to-labor ratio and lower the rate of profit.

Professor C. E. Ferguson, who asserted his faith in neoclassical theory (1963), appealed to the econometricians to find
out whether there is "sufficient substitutability within the
system to establish neoclassical results." Econometrics, at
best, can show what techniques were introduced at the time
when investments were made in the existing stock of means
of production. It cannot show what investments would have
been made if "factor prices" had been different from what
they were. Econometricians, however, ought to be able to compare the capital-to-labor ratio, by any reasonable measure, between different countries; it would certainly be surprising if
they found that, in general, the rate of profit was lowest in
those countries where the capital-to-labor ratio was greatest.
The "Leontief Paradox" arose from a similar misunderstand-
ing. Any rough physical measure of the ratio of capital to

labor, such as horsepower per man employed, showed a higher ratio in the United States than in other industrial countries. Therefore it was supposed that the USA would have a competitive advantage in trade in industries with a high ratio of value of capital to labor. Leontief found that in fact the capital-to-labor ratio was lower in export goods than for imports. This must have meant that relative efficiency in U.S. industries was greatest in those producing both energy and equipment, so that American technology was capital-saving in comparison with that of its rivals.

IV

When all the rubble of disintegrating equilibrium theories has been cleared away, post-Keynesian analysis can come into its own. An economic theory which is seriously intended to apply to reality is neither an ideological doctrine, such as the presumption in favour of laissez-faire, nor a tautology true by definition, such as the so-called quantity formula, $MV = PT$; it is an hypothesis about how an actual economy operates. (See the essay by Basil Moore, page 120.) Hypotheses have to be first examined for logical consistency and *a priori* plausibility, before being applied to historical and contemporary experience. A successful hypothesis is one which suggests new answers to formerly unsolved problems, or frames formerly unrecognized questions.

Post-Keynesian theory has taken over, in the main, the hypotheses suggested by Keynes and by Michal Kalecki and refined and enlarged them to deal with recent experience. The dominant questions at the present time are: Why are the capitalist nations once more suffering from heavy unemployment, and why is it accompanied by inflation instead of by falling prices, as used to be the rule?

Tentative answers can be sketched as follows. The long run of rapid growth and high employment in the industrial economies for twenty-five years after the end of the Second World War, interrupted by only shallow recessions quickly overcome, had many of the characteristics of a boom. Kalecki remarked that the capitalist system causes crises because those crises are useful. A rise in the rate of investment generates a rise in the flow of profits and promotes the employment of labor and the utilization of the pre-existing stock of equipment. This provides a motive for a further rise in investment, but at the same time it is adding to productive capacity. When the growth in the stock of means of production overtakes growth in the flow of profits, the overall rate of profit on capital declines. The inducement to invest is weakened and a recession sets in.

Important innovations in technology and the creation of new commodities open up fresh investment opportunities, and artificial respiration is applied by massive budget deficits. But it would be unreasonable to expect the pace of investment to go on indefinitely rising relative to the growth in the stock of means of production. When it ceases to do so, surplus capacity emerges in the industries producing industrial equipment and durable consumption goods. Here is a hint to explain the situation in the 1970s. A parallel analysis of the financial development of a boom has been made by Hyman Minsky.

To account for the "random shock" which brought the long boom to an end, we must borrow a point from the old-fashioned theory of markets. A rise in the price of a commodity in inelastic demand increases the amount of expenditure on it and so reduces demand for other things. In 1974, the rise in expenditure on oil had deflated worldwide demand for everything else, which led to a fall in industrial output and employment. This setback, surely, would not have introduced a long period of stagnation unless the boom had already exhausted itself by creating an overexpansion of productive capacity (particularly in steel and in automobiles) and an unmanageable accumulation of debt.

One of the most important insights of the Keynesian revolution was a proposition that now seems obvious, that the general level of prices in an industrial economy is determined by the general level of costs, and that the main influence upon costs is to be found in the relation between money-wage rates and output per unit of employment. During the period of almost continuous high employment, there was a general tendency for wage rates to rise relative to productivity.

On top of this, toward the end of the long boom, industrial expansion had overtaken the growth of supplies of many basic materials, causing sharply rising prices in commodity markets, enhanced by speculation. The movement in the two types of costs interact with each other. A rise in material prices leads to an increase in the cost of living relative to money-wage rates and so sets up a demand for a compensating rise. Thus the very success of industrial growth has a built-in tendency to generate inflation, and once inflation has become habitual it continues to feed upon itself after the initiating conditions have disappeared.

The alternative hypothesis that inflation is caused by an excessive creation of money does not pass the first test of logical consistency, for it seems to rely upon the statistical correlation between the stock of money and the flow of money income without explaining what mechanism connects them. It is easy enough to understand how a rise in PT, the money value of the flow of transactions, causes M, the stock of money, to increase, for an increase in working capital calls for an increase of bank credit. And it is easy to understand that if MV fails to increase sufficiently, a restriction of credit will reduce activity, but no one has ever shown how causation is supposed to operate in the reverse direction.

Unfortunately, the financial authorities of the world, including the International Monetary Fund, have adopted the monetarist creed and they insist upon using their authority to impose monetary restriction, which is fairly reliable in reducing real output but has little effect in curbing prices.

In economics, hypotheses cannot be tested by controlled experiments, as in the laboratory sciences, but at least it can be claimed that post-Keynesian theory stands up to the test of experience better than the notions of the monetarists.

V

Although reswitching turned out to be an unnecessary distraction, Sraffa's revival of the classical theory of the rate of profit provides the normal long-period analysis that the post-Keynesian theory requires. It was wrong to class Ricardo with Pigou. Keynes knocked out neoclassical equilibrium and set his argument in historical time. Here he and Ricardo are on the same side.

When technical changes are going on and new commodities are being introduced, the clearcut distinctions of Sraffa's model cannot be drawn, but the principle remains that the clue to a theory of distribution is to be found in the relations between technical conditions and the share of profit in the flow of the value of output.

It is fashionable nowadays to argue that the great corporations can make their selling prices what they please, and that their policy is to set gross margins at the level which is expected to yield the funds that they need to carry out their investment plans; but it would be no less plausible to argue that investment plans are influenced by the gross profits actually realized. In either case, obviously, the most successful firms are those that make the greatest gross profits and carry out the most rapid accumulation of capital.

For industry as a whole, higher gross margins in a given state of effective demand do not generate a higher level of profits. At any phase of development, an overall reduction in gross margins would not reduce total profits but would raise real wages and increase employment.

All these questions remain to be investigated. The writers of these papers, throwing off the paralysis of neoclassical equilibrium, are exploring, from various points of view, the problems of prices, employment, accumulation, distribution, growth, and stagnation in the actual, historical evolution of an everchanging world. In the nature of the case, definitive answers cannot be found quickly. There is plenty of work still to do.

*A Guide to
Post-Keynesian
Economics*

ALFRED S. EICHNER

Introduction

Ever since the marginalist revolution of the late nineteenth century, economic theory has become more and more elegant as a set of axiomatic statements about resource allocation under competitive market conditions. The precision with which assumptions are stated, the subtlety with which the logic is then pursued, and the rigor with which a proof is finally adduced all seem to support the claim of economics to be the Euclidian geometry, if not the physics, of the social sciences.

At the same time, economic theory has become less and less useful to anyone hoping to understand phenomena of the real world, such as economic growth, cyclical fluctuations, inflation, poverty, unemployment, underdevelopment—or even business success. Public officials, private businessmen, students, and ordinary citizens all find economic theory divorced from the reality they need to comprehend. It is this contrast between its elegance and its relevance that underlies the current crisis in economics—a crisis which threatens the discipline's reputation as a science.

Fortunately, economics encompasses more than just axiomatic statements about resource allocation. A large number of economists, disenchanted by what they regard as the vacuity of economic theory, have come to disdain the use of any conceptual framework, preferring to work instead as pure empiricists. Some of the quantitative studies they have produced, on demand elasticities, cost functions, mark-up pricing, the functional distribution of income, the labor component of foreign-traded goods, and other technical matters, have not only added significantly to our knowledge about the economy, but have also helped reveal the considerable disparity between theory and reality. Nevertheless, this empirical work has not been entirely free of conceptual limitations for, if nothing else, the choice of what to measure is an *a priori* judgment.

A much smaller group of economists has responded to the vacuity of the prevailing economic theory in quite a different way. They have attempted to reformulate the core of that theory in a more realistic manner. Though they are hardly a cohesive group—indeed, no more so than the rival neoclassical school—the work of these economists does have certain important features in common. Moreover, as the group has expanded in size and the argument has extended to areas outside the core of economic theory, the awareness of what those common features are has also grown. In deference to the economist responsible for the first major break in orthodox theory, but also mindful of how incomplete the break has been, the group prefers to be known as the post-Keynesians. Its members represent the coming together of several dissident traditions within economics—that of the American institutionalists and the continental Marxists, as well as that of Keynes' closest associates. Their work, taken together, potentially offers a comprehensive and coherent alternative to the prevailing orthodoxy in economic theory, an orthodoxy which, because of its lack of relevance, stands as the principal obstacle to intelligent economic policy.

What follows in this introductory essay will be an attempt to specify the features common to all the work that falls under this post-Keynesian rubric. Once these distinguishing characteristics have been identified, it will become clear that the term "post-Keynesian" applies to the work of many more economists than are now even aware that such an alternative body of theory exists; many of them are post-Keynesians without knowing it. Indeed, it will become clear that many of the anomalous findings of the pure empiricists simply confirm the greater relevance of the post-Keynesian paradigm for understanding the real world.

The subsequent essays in this volume will indicate how the post-Keynesian framework leads to a different type of analysis in various subject areas of economics—macrodynamics, pricing, income distribution, money, tax incidence, international trade, labor, and natural resources. Both the major theoretical points of difference between post-Keynesian and neoclassical theory and the resulting policy implications will be brought out. This introductory essay, after first explaining how the post-Keynesian paradigm emerged from the dissatisfaction of some economists with the old one, will present in summary fashion the distinguishing characteristics of this body of work.

The emergence of post-Keynesian theory

No sooner had the marginalist revolution in economic theory taken hold around the turn of the century than certain economists began to criticize the new concepts for their abstraction from the reality of contemporary institutions. Both the members of the historical school in Germany and Thorstein Veblen in this country were in the vanguard of the attack.

The response of Alfred Marshall, the holder of the only chair in economics in one of the only two major British universities then offering a degree in economics, was ambivalent. On the one hand, he was convinced of the greater analytical power of the new marginalist theories. They appealed to his mathematical frame of mind and to his desire to transform the study of political economy into the science of economics. Indeed, the *Principles*, which he first brought out in 1890, presented the most sophisticated exposition of marginalist analysis that had yet been developed, and the succeeding seven editions would reign as the dominant textbook in the English-speaking countries until well after World War II. On the other hand, Marshall was aware of his position as the heir to the Ricardian tradition in economics. While some of this tradition could be synthesized with the new marginalist theories, some of it could not. Moreover, as a believer in the evolutionary ideas of Darwin, Marshall was not entirely at ease with the static framework of the marginalist analysis. Indeed, as Marshall was aware, that framework was an incongruous vehicle for the "study of mankind in the ordinary business of life," including the "struggle for survival" among business firms.

These ambivalences were never wholly resolved—certainly not in the *Principles*, where chapters providing historical and institutional description are interspersed with chapters of marginalist analysis, along with a clear warning as to the limitations of the latter. As a result, the neoclassical theory that gained ascendancy in Great Britain and the rest of the English-speaking world was not as abstracted from reality as the neoclassical theory that was developed on the continent by Walras and his followers. The contrast was reflected in the difference between the time-specific (short- and long-run), partial equilibrium analysis of the Marshallians and the timeless, general equilibrium analysis of the Walrasians. With this point in mind, it is easier to understand the transformation of Keynes as a theorist from a minor Marshallian specializing in monetary matters to the most effective challenger of orthodoxy since the triumph of marginalist analysis. For in Keynes, the separate Ricardian and institutionalist sides of Marshall finally burst through in a new type of theoretical synthesis, one finally responsive to the political problems of the day.

It has become commonplace to speak of the "Keynesian Revolution." Yet it is not clear that Keynes was the most important of the Keynesians or that *The General Theory* produced the revolution in economic theory it is credited with. Of course, in terms of prestige, Keynes was pre-eminent. His position at Cambridge, his editorship of the *Economic Journal*, and his service in government combined to give him an audience for any ideas he might put forward that no other contemporary economist could command. Still, Keynes was but the leading figure among a group of like-minded individuals who would put economics on a wholly new path of development and make the university on the Cam the intellectual home base for dissidents from orthodox theory the world over—at least until recently. There were, besides Keynes, his younger colleagues and kindred spirits associated with the famed "Circus" at Cambridge—Richard Kahn, who had contributed the multiplier concept, and Joan Robinson, with her work on imperfect competition. There were the younger scholars from outside Cambridge—Nicholas Kaldor, who would later move to Cambridge from the London School, and Roy Harrod, who would remain at Oxford. As a peer of Keynes himself at Cambridge, there was Piero Sraffa who, after unsettling Marshallian microeconomic theory in 1926 with his article in the *Economic Journal* on returns to scale, had embarked on the task of restoring Ricardo's reputation in economics. And finally there was Michal Kalecki, the Polish Marxist who arrived in England shortly after *The General Theory* was published with his own, prior version of the same model and who, through Joan Robinson, soon became part of the same group.

It is difficult to say who, in the succeeding forty years, exerted the greater influence on the development of post-Keynesian theory, Keynes himself or Kalecki. Together, they represent the origins of the two separate strands in classical Keynesianism—one strand emerging from the monetary perspective of Keynes and the other from the real sector analysis of Kalecki. The first emphasizes the uncertainties surrounding investment in a monetarized economy, the second the distributional and other effects of investment and savings, with both elements essential for a complete analysis of production over time in a money-using economic system. Ironically, it was the real sector analysis of Kalecki that became the basis for further work at Cambridge while Keynes' monetary perspective would be sustained elsewhere—by G. L. S. Shackle in Great Britain and by Sidney Weintraub, Paul Davidson, and Hyman P. Minsky in the United States. Moreover, the version of Keynesian theory that was brought to the United States by Alvin Hansen and Lawrence Klein, and which became the dominant version of the theory in this country, was also closer in spirit to Kalecki's simple methematical model than to *The General Theory* itself—even though, in a characteristically American way, it totally ignored Kalecki's emphasis on distributional effects.

The key contributions

The first step in the development of post-Keynesian, as distinct from a Keynesian analysis, came with Harrod's work in the 1930s on growth dynamics. The prevailing theory in economics was static rather than dynamic. This meant that it served primarily to explain how the economic system, assumed to be initially at rest, reached a new resting point when and if it was disturbed from without. What was necessary, Harrod argued, was a body of theory to explain what caused the observable movement of the economic system to change over time. In response to this need, Harrod developed his fundamental equation, better known to American economists as the Harrod-Domar formula, in which the growth rate, as the dependent variable, is determined by the propensity to save and the incremental capital/output ratio. But it was not until nearly two decades later that Harrod's pioneering effort to develop a dynamic analysis bore fruit in the emergence of a relatively robust post-Keynesian theory.

In 1956 two key writings appeared. One was a book, *The Accumulation of Capital*, by Robinson; the other an article, "Alternative Theories of Distribution," by Kaldor in the *Review of Economic Studies*. Together, they mark the beginning of a distinctly post-Keynesian body of literature in economics. Both drew on the distinction between wages and profits in the work of Kalecki (and, through him, in Marx) to explain an essential aspect of growth dynamics, one inextricably linked to the distribution of income. The point was that an increase in the growth rate, because of the higher level of investment that it implied, would necessarily be accompanied by a larger share of profits in national income, thus leaving workers relatively worse off. Both of these published pieces, however, received little attention from economists outside the Cambridge coterie. Indeed Robinson, feeling that perhaps the fault was hers for making the argument in *The Accumulation of Capital* too parsimonious, subsequently wrote her *Essays in the Theory of Economic Growth* in explication, but the response from other economists was no better.

The fact was that at the same time Keynes' one-time associates and followers at Cambridge were attempting to enlarge upon his break with orthodox theory, others within the economics profession were working to contain the Keynesian heresy. This was especially true in the United States, which had largely replaced Great Britain as the dominant world power. There, among liberal economists, a new "neoclassical synthesis" had emerged, based on the work of Paul Samuelson, who both translated the received theory into mathematics and wrote a popular textbook for beginning students. In this exegesis, the Keynesian macroeconomic model was simply grafted onto the prevailing microeconomic theory, with the distinction between the Marshallian and Walrasian approaches lost. The fusion was carried out despite the lack of compatibility between the Keynesian macroeconomic model, with its emphasis on the income effects from changes in investment and other discretionary spending, and the prevailing microeconomic theory, with its emphasis on the substitution effects resulting from price changes. The Keynesian arguments, it was held, applied only in the short run when various market imperfections prevented the neoclassical theory's adjustment mechanisms from taking full effect and the resulting unemployment was likely to prove politically unacceptable. Over the longer run, however, especially with the government committed to using the new mode of analysis to deal with the short-run unemployment problem, the pre-Keynesian theory could still be relied upon. Indeed, this was the underlying assumption of the neoclassical growth model formulated by Robert Solow, Samuelson's colleague at MIT (and by Trevor Swan in Australia), in 1956, the same year in which both *The Accumulation of Capital* and "Alternative Theories of Distribution" appeared.

Politically, the neoclassical synthesis led to the policies, in the 1960s, of "fine-tuning" an American economy presumed to be fundamentally stable without the need for more drastic forms of intervention. This political program met its debacle over the problem of inflation, thus precipitating the current crisis in economics. For there was nothing in the neoclassical synthesis to suggest how the goals of full employment and price stability could be achieved conjointly, thus avoiding the need to make a Phillipsian choice between the two—or even to explain how recession and inflation could occur simultaneously, as they did throughout the 1970s. It is the growing lack of confidence in all theoretical models that marks the current crisis in economics. In the resulting confusion, less liberal economists have sought to strip the neoclassical synthesis of its Keynesian trappings, arguing for a return to the monetarism from which Keynes, with his training under Marshall, struggled to escape in the 1930s. Yet, what to other economists is a growing disparity between theory and experience is, to those economists who have reoriented their work along post-Keynesian lines, simply confirmation of the conceptual framework they employ. In particular, the simultaneous occurrence of inflation and recession is what they would expect under modern economic conditions when neither price nor wage setting depends solely on impersonal market forces.

The number of economists who have consciously and openly made this shift in paradigm is, as already indicated, quite small—the size of the group reflecting the resistance to their ideas from the established centers of orthodoxy, situated both in the leading graduate training centers in this country and in the leading economics journals. But the number of economists who are either unfamiliar with this alternative to neoclassical theory or who, having come to some of the same ideas themselves, are unaware of the larger body of work within which those ideas fall is much larger. Perhaps they even constitute a majority of the economics profession when those who specialize in applied fields are taken into account.

The essential elements

What, then, is the nature of post-Keynesian theory?

Some of the answer has already been given in the brief historical overview of the emergence of post-Keynesian theory from the work of Keynes' closest associates at Cambridge University both before and immediately after World War II; the rest of the answer will be found in the subsequent essays in this collection. At this point it will suffice to indicate only some of the most general features which distinguish post-Keynesian theory from the opposing neoclassical orthodoxy.

First, post-Keynesian theory offers an explanation of economic growth and income distribution—with the two viewed as being directly linked to one another. The key determinant is the same for both. This is the rate of investment, whether measured against total national income or viewed as the percentage change over time. Thus, in place of the relative price variable which is the focal point of a neoclassical analysis, post-Keynesian theory makes investment the key determinant. This follows from an underlying belief that in a dynamic, expanding economy (paraphrasing neoclassical terminology), the income effects produced by investment and other sources of growth far outweigh the substitution effects resulting from price movements. That is, changes in demand, both aggregate and sectoral, are due more to changes in income than to changes in relative prices. Indeed, the importance attached to income—as opposed to substitution— effects is a sensitive barometer of just how post-Keynesian, or even Keynesian, any particular piece of analysis is. This is not to say that post-Keynesian theory ignores substitution effects altogether. It's merely that it refuses to view these effects as the only, or even the most significant, part of the dynamic process. In contrast, the neoclassical theory usually eliminates, by assumption, any possible income effects. Indeed, this is the purpose served by positing long-run full employment in most neoclassical models. The post-Keynesian theory is less arbitrary in this respect: it recognizes that income effects will dominate in the short run and will be no less important than the substitution effects over longer time periods.

Second, post-Keynesian theory is formulated with the dominant economic fact of the past several centuries clearly in mind. This is the continuous, though uneven, expansion of the various national economies over time. Thus, even if no change is posited in either the determinants or parameters of the model, the economic system is still depicted as proceeding along some secular growth path. This view of the economic system as being constantly in motion stands in sharp contrast to both the general equilibrium and partial equilibrium versions of neoclassical theory, whereby even if a change occurs in the determinants or parameters of the model, the system is still viewed as coming to rest at some fixed level of activity. In fact, as already suggested, this view of an economic system constantly in motion is what delineates post-Keynesian theory from the standard macroeconomic models based on a vulgar Keynesianism. The "neoclassical" growth models, while they cannot be faulted on these same grounds, suffer from another type of defect.

In depicting an economic system that is expanding continuously over time, post-Keynesian theory recognizes the need to distinguish between the factors responsible for the secular growth of output, and those responsible for the cyclical movements around that trend line—even if at least one of the factors, the rate of investment, is the same. This methodological principle gives rise to the distinction between the post-Keynesian long-period and short-period analysis. The long-period analysis, in isolating the determinants of secular expansion, does not presume, as a neoclassical growth model does, that market forces alone are sufficient eventually to bring the economy back to the warranted growth path—should it ever stray from that path—the one on which the economy can expand at a constant, steady rate. Quite the contrary, the determinants of the secular growth rate are first identified so as to bring out even more clearly the separate factors responsible for the constant deviations around the trend line. In thus denying that cyclical fluctuations, whether caused by exogenous shocks or not, are necessarily self-correcting, post-Keynesian theory remains true to its Keynesian antecedents. In contrast, the "neoclassical" growth models simply assume away the need for any short-period analysis, even though it is the short period that gives rise to all the serious problems of the economy.

Third, post-Keynesian theory is meant to describe an economic system with advanced credit and other monetary institutions—all of which play a fundamental role in the dynamic processes being analyzed. This is in contrast to the neoclassical model, including its monetarist offshoots, in which money does not matter insofar as real output is concerned, only insofar as the secular rate of inflation is concerned. It is the existence of money, produced partly in response to credit needs, that makes meaningful the distinction in post-Keynesian models between savings and investment or, more broadly, taking into account the role of consumer durable and government expenditures, between discretionary income and discretionary spending. It is, moreover, the elasticity of credit, as the banking system either activates or sterilizes idle balances, depending on the demand for loans, that prevents the full brunt of any changes in economic activity from being felt on the real side of production. If a sudden spurt in government expenditures or some other form of discretionary spending should give rise to a sharp increase in the demand for cash, the commercial banking system is likely to use whatever excess reserves it has to meet the needs of customers for additional credit. And if the banking system's reserves should become stretched to the limit, there are still other sources of credit that can be tapped—for example, by stretching out the repayment of old debt, or increasing trade credit. In the reverse situation, when a decline in discretionary spending has led to a modest business downturn, the commercial banking system is likely to find its reserves building up again as the demand for cash and credit declines. Indeed, the build-up of reserves will largely sterilize any excess flow of funds into the commercial banking system. Of course, if the downturn in business activity is severe enough to impair confidence in the financial structure, then one will observe a quite different result, namely, a liquidity crisis, as the decline in asset values progresses to the point where it undermines the whole basis for banks extending credit.

Even though modern banking and other credit institutions are thus designed to be accommodating to discretionary spending decisions, it is possible, through central bank policies, to make them less so. In that event, money does matter —affecting not only the amplitude of the current business cycle but the secular growth of real output as well. Money matters because without it purchases, especially discretionary ones, cannot be made. And if purchases cannot be made, aggregate demand will fall. Even if some discretionary spending is only temporarily delayed for lack of liquid funds— except at a prohibitive rate of interest—the economy's actual growth path will be different from what it would otherwise be. In the extreme case, when credit is cut off entirely and cash cannot be raised from any source, the result, again, is a liquidity crisis—though now, under the posited circumstances, as a direct result of central bank policies.

Fourth, post-Keynesian theory has no trouble recognizing the existence of multinational corporations and the somewhat less powerful national trade unions. Within the industrial core of a modern, technologically advanced economy, both prices and wages are assumed to be "administered"— that is, they are quoted by the supplier on a take-it-or-leave-it basis, even if sales are sometimes made off list. The prices that are thus quoted become parameters determining the rate of savings, or discretionary income, within the business and household sectors, just as the tax rates imposed by government are parameters determining the revenue in-flows, or discretionary income, of the public sector. The higher the price level in the oligopolistic core of the economy, costs and other factors remaining unchanged, the greater will be the rate of cash flow and thus the larger the volume of internally generated savings.

Post-Keynesian theory takes into account not only this system of administered, or seller-quoted, prices in the industrial sector, but also the system of more flexible prices which prevails in world commodity markets. Indeed, the interplay between the two sectors, one oligopolistic and the other competitive, is an important part of the inflationary process. This microeconomic base of post-Keynesian theory stands in sharp contrast to the neoclassical model, the conclusions of which depend critically on the assumption that all suppliers of goods and labor services are price-takers in competitive markets. In a post-Keynesian analysis, competition need involve no more than a continual effort by business firms to exploit the most profitable investment opportunities. It is only competition in this limited sense that generally prevails throughout the world —a fact that the classical economists clearly recognized.

Fifth, and finally, post-Keynesian theory is concerned with the dynamic behavior of actual economic systems. It is not limited, as neoclassical theory is, to the analysis of resource allocation under hypothetical market conditions. By thus refusing to limit its purview to competitive market processes —it can encompass both noncompetitive market processes and non-market forms of allocation—post-Keynesian theory is able to look at the economic system with fewer intellectual blinders while still providing a workable model to explain the system's laws of motion. And because it does not have to make unwarranted assumptions about the nature of economic institutions, it is a model more consistent with the knowledge derived from the other social sciences.

Policy implications

For many interested parties, the critical question will be, what are the policy implications of post-Keynesian theory? Are they radical, liberal, or conservative? This question probably cannot be answered to the full satisfaction of anyone who might ask it. Still, some response can be given.

The shift from neoclassical to post-Keynesian economics

resembles previous shifts in scientific paradigms. While the change is occurring, it is easier to identify the outmoded concepts that are likely to be swept away than to anticipate all the implications, political as well as intellectual, of this new mode of analysis. For the incipient paradigm is more a program of research, with unproductive lines of inquiry roped off, than a fully developed body of knowledge. Those implications that can already be foreseen are likely to be disconcerting across a wide spectrum of political opinion. Conservatives, for example, will not be happy with the conclusion that the distribution of income can be significantly altered without impairing the productivity of the system. Liberals will not be happy with the notion that competitive markets are not essential to the efficient working of the system. And radicals will not be happy with the idea that the system may be stable even without a fundamental transformation of institutions. Still, one should not exaggerate the degree of consensus even on these broad points. At this stage in its development, post-Keynesian theory remains far from a settled orthodoxy.

If there is perhaps one point on which economists with a post-Keynesian perspective are likely to agree, it is that inflation cannot be controlled through conventional instruments of fiscal and monetary policy. This is because they regard inflation as resulting, not necessarily from any "excess demand" for goods, but rather from a more fundamental conflict over the distribution of available income and output. The conventional policy instruments, by curtailing the level of economic activity, simply reduce the amount of income and output available for distribution, thereby heightening the social conflict underlying the inflationary process. They do not moderate, except most imperfectly, the income claims against available output so that the growth of nominal income over time will be equal to the growth of real income, without the need for rising prices to bring the two into balance. It is for this reason that post-Keynesian economists, instead of asking whether an incomes policy is necessary, have generally moved on to the question of how an incomes policy can be made to work effectively and equitably.

JOHN CORNWALL

Macrodynamics

The terms macrodynamics and macrodynamic theory are used by economists today to designate the area of economics that deals with the development of capitalist economies over time. The aim is to describe and explain both business cycles and economic growth patterns in developed market economies.

In their early stages, macrodynamic theories were developed on a "grand" and "magnificent" scale by writers such as Malthus, Ricardo, and Marx in an attempt to discover more than just the "laws" of economic development. Social, political, and cultural developments were also considered in a tradition that continued into the twentieth century with Schumpeter and Veblen. The modern versions of macrodynamic theory trace their origins to the work of the English economist, Roy Harrod, and of the American economist, Evsey Domar, in the 1930s and 1940s. While much narrower in scope than the work of their famous predecessors, these studies have been no less influential in terms of the vast number of other studies they have spawned.

Two points of interest for the future development of macrodynamics flowed from these writings. First, Keynes in *The General Theory* concentrated on the income-generating, or multiplier effects, of investment—that is, the process whereby an increase in investment leads to an increase in income which will be some multiple of the investment increase. Naturally, the rise in spending stimulates a rise in employment as well. However, investment, even if it is simply maintained at the same rate, adds continuously to the capacity of the economy to produce goods, since it is an addition to the capital stock. This means, therefore, that in order to generate sufficient aggregate demand to maintain full use of the total productive capacity of the economy, it is not enough for investment to be a large but fixed amount. Investment must be growing at a certain rate in order to generate the growth in demand needed to keep the economy's expanding capital stock fully utilized.

Second, from this recognition of the dual role of investment, whereby it generates demand and also adds to capacity, there developed a belief that a capitalist system might be inherently unstable. The problem is simply posed: Why should the growth of demand that results from a certain rate of growth of investment (the multiplier effect) be just equal to the rate of growth of capacity which results from this same growth of investment? Why, for example, might the rate of growth of investment not give rise to a lesser rate of growth of demand than of capacity? If this should happen, the resulting excess capacity can be expected to force the economy into a recession. Even if demand and capacity are growing at the same rate, this may be less than the rate of growth of the labor force (plus a possible adjustment for the growth in labor productivity, as determined by the rate of technological change). A rise in the rate of unemployment is then likely to follow. In an analogous manner the rate of growth of investment, and therefore of demand, could outstrip the resulting growth of capacity and the labor force, thus creating an inflationary situation.

The rate of growth of demand (and investment) that is just enough to keep all capital fully utilized was referred to by Harrod as the "warranted" rate of growth; that which was just sufficient to employ a growing labor force, after taking into account any increased labor productivity, was referred to as the "natural" or "potential" rate of growth. The problem posed by what has come to be called Harrod-Domar analysis can be rephrased as follows: Is it likely or even possible for a capitalist economy actually to grow at a rate equal to the warranted and natural rates, thereby maintaining the full use of all capital and the full employment of all labor? To many, a negative response seemed the only appropriate one.

The neoclassical parable

Coming as these developments did so soon after the worst of the Great Depression, the Harrod-Domar framework seemed to provide certain insights into why capitalism had experienced, and would continue to experience, serious depressions. This partly explains why the impact of these studies on the future development of macrodynamic theory was so substantial. The 1950s, especially, witnessed a vast outpouring of theories and models that could generate recessions as well as booms, as part of the natural development of a capitalist system. These theories and models, for reasons soon to be made clear, would be considered as part of the Keynesian tradition. However, during the mid-1950s there also developed a totally different macrodynamic tradition that stood in sharp contrast to this post-Keynesian mode of analysis. This was the development of neoclassical growth theory, an approach that has dominated macrodynamic theory to this day.

The intention of the early neoclassical growth theorists was to determine the sources of instability in the Harrod-Domar analysis and to see in what ways stability could be restored. In retrospect, it is clear that these were important questions to answer and in many respects the results constituted a real advance in macrodynamics: assumptions were made more explicit; "price effects" were incorporated; greater rigor was introduced, and reasonable answers were found. But having achieved these gains, the proponents of neoclassical growth theory, consciously or unconsciously, went on to establish a framework that completely altered the orientation of macrodynamics. Instead of developing a theory to explain why economic growth and business cycles have historically gone hand in hand, the neoclassicists attempted to analyze the sources of economic growth as though the problem of cyclical fluctuations did not exist. Thus the growth theory that emerged in the 1950s represented a step backward from the earlier Keynesian revolution in economics—indeed, even a step backward from the vulgar Keynesianism propounded in most introductory textbooks.

Consider the following elements of what can be regarded as the hard core of neoclassical growth theory, that is, when the theory has been stripped of its mathematical outer covering to reveal its underlying premises and purposes.

1. The main points of interest in macrodynamics are to determine (a) whether or not in any theory or model there exists a situation in which all the relevant economic variables such as output, the capital stock, investment, and labor can grow at the same contant rate; and (b) whether there is a tendency for these same variables to resume this constant rate of growth should the economy be displaced from its warranted and natural growth path.

2. The factors that determine long-term growth rates are all on the supply side; they are the factors underlying the rate of growth of the labor force and the rate of technological change. However, what determines the rate at which these supply factors grow is almost never explained.

3. Demand plays a passive role; if the economy is capable of steady, stable growth, the rate of growth of demand merely adjusts to the more fundamental supply factors just mentioned. Aggregate demand is always "just right": all units of every factor are assumed to be fully employed. Largely be-

cause of this assumption, the actual growth rate and what was earlier referred to as the warranted rate of growth are readily brought into line with the natural rate of growth. This results from the workings of a price mechanism which behaves so efficiently that whenever there might be the slightest tendency for any units of capital or labor to be unemployed, relative factor prices adjust, inducing a return to the full employment of all capital and labor. In short, neoclassical growth analysis does not concern itself with problems of inadequate demand, the business cycle or unemployment. The economy is never, in this sense, in disequilibrium. Thus, neoclassical macrodynamics can be described simply as neoclassical growth theory.

4. Full employment output or aggregate supply can be analyzed in terms of a simple production function, one which relates the total output of an economy to the inputs of capital and labor. This functional relationship assumes "constant returns to scale"; i.e., if all inputs are increased by a certain percentage, then output increases by the same percentage.

5. Whatever fixed proportion of income the recipients of income choose to save, that proportion will determine the share of aggregate output which is invested. Moreover, whatever the size of this investment share of aggregate output, the long-run growth rate of the economy will be unaffected. This is because the long-run growth rate depends on the supply factors cited above, so that a higher rate of investment may lead to more capital-intensive methods of production or even a temporary deviation from the warranted and natural rates of growth, but not a change in those growth rates.

6. Neoclassical theory in all of its forms shows a strong tendency to reduce the economic (as distinguished from the mathematical) complexity of the analysis, doing so by holding the institutional framework constant. This is accomplished by assuming that consumer tastes and production technologies remain more or less unchanged. In neoclassical growth theory,

the above assumption is introduced in two ways. If the economy is viewed from a total or overall perspective, both the aggregate production and the aggregate savings functions are posited as being fixed. If the economy is disaggregated into sectors, the growth process is treated as one in which all sectors of the economy grow at the same rate, together producing a total output whose composition never changes. This unchanged composition of output depends on an unchanged collection of technologies or production functions.

7. Perfect competition prevails in all markets. There are no monopoly elements and all persons have perfect knowledge of past, present, and future events. Real wages are equalized across jobs and rates of return on capital are equalized across firms.

8. Since innovations, that is, the introduction of new technologies or new goods, are excluded from consideration, since the portion of output saved and invested is determined by income recipients, and since perfect competition prevails, the only role for the businessman is to coordinate production —for example, substituting capital for labor when the relative price of capital falls, and vice versa.

The post-Keynesian alternative

The evolution of neoclassical macrodynamics since the mid-1950s has been characterized by an increased mathematical sophistication and complexity. Little effort has been made to extend the analysis, however, and thus to incorporate most of the important economic phenomena to be found in the real world—trade unions, oligopolies, unemployment, uncertainty, variations in demand pressures, the continuous introduction of new technologies and goods. As a result, neoclassical macrodynamics has failed to develop in such a way as to answer the kinds of questions raised by macrodynamic theorists since the early nineteenth century: why one country grows more rapidly than another; why growth accelerates in some periods and not in others; what the likely patterns of capitalist development are; and why unemployment is more of a problem in one country or period than another.

While neoclassical growth theory has dominated the journals and discussions during the postwar period, an alternative paradigm or view of macrodynamics, one decidedly more Keynesian in outlook, has remained alive. In some universities such as Cambridge it even flourished, based on the important contributions of Nicholas Kaldor and Joan Robinson. Like neoclassical growth theory, its modern origins can be traced to the Harrod-Domar analysis (to some extent) but no two traditions could be more different in their conception of the proper study of macrodynamic processes. Although there is no rigid orthodoxy, certain common elements have emerged which allow one at least to outline this post-Keynesian conception of macrodynamics. What follows is a description of the post-Keynesian paradigm that stresses those aspects that, to this writer, bring out its strengths most clearly, while highlighting the weaknesses of neoclassical growth theory. The contrast is formulated first in general terms and then in more detail.

The post-Keynesian view of macrodynamics sees a capitalist system as one growing over time but in an uneven manner. Of central concern is the question why these growth rates differ between countries or at different periods of time within a country. In addition, given the stress on the unevenness of the growth process, there is the question why a capitalist economy is characterized by short-run cyclical fluctuations in output and employment, with investment playing such a key role in generating these cycles. The first question has given rise to the post-Keynesian long-period analysis; the second, to the post-Keynesian short period analysis.

Because short-run fluctuations are not ruled out, post-Keynesian macrodynamics is able to highlight the view that a capitalist system is usually in some kind of disequilibrium. It is then but a short step to a key concern of post-Keynesian macrodynamics: What is the adjustment mechanism in capitalist economies that works to limit these short-run fluctuations so that unemployment rates rarely reach, say, double-digit figures? Any number of empirical considerations suggest it is not the price mechanism alone that produces this result. And the collapse of the 1930s suggests that there is no automatic self-correcting mechanism that can always be counted on.

The different assumptions

In one sense, then, post-Keynesian macrodynamics has been concerned, as has neoclassical macrodynamics, with the nature of long-run equilibrium and its stability. It also seeks to discover whether the actual growth rate of an economy tends to equal what were earlier referred to as the warranted and natural rates of growth. However, as just indicated, this has been viewed as only the beginning of the analysis in post-Keynesian macrodynamics. The central concern has been to explain why growth rates differ and why cyclical fluctuations occur.

In an effort to solve these types of problems, post-Keynesian macrodynamics has been forced to discard most of the basic assumptions of neoclassical analysis. Two of the more important are the latter's assumptions of given tastes and given technologies. In so doing, post-Keynesian theorists have been able to view the process of growth as one of "qualitative change" (to use Schumpeter's term), whereby the composition of output and the methods of producing that output are constantly shifting. Thus, in the course of real-life processes of growth, as per capita income rises, demand shifts to new goods as consumer tastes change, inducing a shift in the distribution of resources and the development of new technologies to produce the goods now in greater demand. By seeking to highlight these critical aspects of qualitative change during a given era, post-Keynesian macrodynamics seeks to infuse the analysis with a "sense of history."

This view of growth as unbalanced, with some industries in decline and others booming, has several other dimensions. The rise of new industries, new firms, and new products involves the introduction of new technologies (in addition to changing consumer tastes). Post-Keynesian macrodynamics emphasizes the variability of technology in this and at least two other senses. Post-Keynesian analysis allows for and indeed even emphasizes variable returns to scale: if a firm, an industry, or the economy increases its use of both labor and capital by, say, 10 percent, output may increase by more than, less than, or exactly by 10 percent. In addition, the kinds of technologies and the degrees of mechanization can and usually will vary across and within sectors of the economy. A common feature of even the most advanced capitalist economy is the coexistence of highly mechanized firms employing the latest technologies alongside technologically backward, inefficient firms, not only in the same sector of the economy (manufacturing, for example), but often in the same industry. As might be expected, profit rates (and wage rates) thus vary quite widely across sectors in real economies. Post-Keynesian macrodynamics incorporates into its analysis these related phenomena.

The fact that growth is a process involving continuous change in consumer tastes and production technology points up again a profound difference between the post-Keynesian and neoclassical views as to the importance of investment. In the latter view, an increase in the share of output devoted to investment cannot permanently increase the rate at which the economy grows. Post-Keynesian theory, in contrast, emphasizes that new technologies can seldom be introduced without large doses of investment. Since the process of growth is viewed as one of rising per capita income, with the composition of final demand changing as consumers move up through the "hierarchy of goods" defined by the relative income elasticities of demand for different items, it follows that the new technologies required by the changing composition of final demand must necessarily be embodied in the new capital goods being purchased. Other things being equal, the bigger the share of output devoted to investment, the more rapidly will this growth process unfold.

As might be expected, this changing composition of demand and continuous introduction of new technologies—largely through investment—will have a tendency to proceed at an uneven pace. This partly explains the uneven nature of the growth process discussed earlier. No matter what share of output is devoted to the production of investment goods, the unbalanced nature of the growth process that is taking place will inevitably lead to fluctuations in the level of investment and thus in the rate of expansion. These cyclical movements are what the post-Keynesian short-period analysis is intended to explain.

Where do the savings to finance large investment outlays come from? In post-Keynesian economics there is no presumption that these savings are limited to the proportion of income that capitalists and other heads of households choose not to spend on current consumption needs—certainly not in the case of the business investment which is the key to rapid growth. In real life, most household savings flow into the housing market and therefore are not available to finance business investment. As Kalecki emphasized forty years ago, the savings used to finance the latter are to a large extent generated internally. This is easily enough accomplished when sales are booming and capacity is being strained. But even under less favorable circumstances, business pricing policy plays a critical role, for profit margins can be increased (within limits) to provide the additional funds needed for investment. The implication is that savings as a share of total national income are to a large extent determined by the business sector, especially the larger oligopolistic firms. This suggests that the savings (and investment) ratio can be and is highly variable, in both the short and the long run.

Taking the argument one step further, changes in the savings ratio can be looked upon as the alternative to the change in relative factor prices relied upon in neoclassical models to explain the stability of advanced market economies. Both devices function essentially as adjustment mechanisms for bringing demand and supply back into line once an economy deviates from its warranted and natural growth rates. The changes in the savings ratio are emphasized in post-Keynesian models because it is felt that in the real world this adjustment mechanism plays by far the more important role.

It should be clear from the above discussion, emphasizing the importance of new technologies, of firms responding to changing consumer tastes, and of the connection between pricing and investment policies, that post-Keynesian macrodynamics views the entrepreneur—or the entrepreneurial element in any large-scale organization—as being central to the growth process. The neoclassical world of fixed tastes and technologies, fixed savings and investment ratios, and perfect information about the past, present, and future course of events is a world where entrepreneurship has little place. Rather it is the world of the accountant, with passive response to changes in relative prices being the rule as production is merely coordinated rather than initiated.

In summary, post-Keynesian macrodynamics can be seen as an attempt to incorporate both the institutional framework of an advanced market economy and the manner in which this institutional framework changes over time into the explanation of growth and cyclical processes. Unlike neoclassical macrodynamics, it strives to encompass the real world of uncertainty, oligopolies, new products and technologies, a world in which the "human element" is reflected in the quality of the entrepreneurial class. The view of post-Keynesian economists is that only by incorporating these elements into the analysis can macrodynamics even begin to suggest solutions to the problems of the real world.

Policy implications

What are the implications for public policy following from these two different paradigms? An answer to this question serves to bring out in another way the relative explanatory power of the two approaches. Neoclassical growth analysis lends itself very poorly to policy prescriptions. Since it does not deal with the business cycle or allow for unemployment, it is unable to formulate anti-cyclical or full employment policies based on analysis. Furthermore, since growth rates are ultimately determined by unexplained factors, it cannot formulate policies for influencing growth rates either.

These decidedly negative conclusions flow automatically from the very nature of the theoretical structure of neoclassical growth theory and the kinds of questions it has sought to answer. A preoccupation with determining the mathematical properties of models has led to a neglect of their empirical content. Hence, the inability to deal with policy issues.

In contrast, the theoretical structure of post-Keynesian macrodynamics has developed out of a desire to explain differences in the relative performance of national economies. Only to the extent that it can achieve this aim can it aid in policy formulation. For example, post-Keynesian macrodynamics stresses the key role of investment in generating cycles as well as in determining growth rates. This immediately suggests the first priority in considering stabilization, employment and growth policies. Steady and rapid growth of aggregate output at high levels of employment requires steady and rapid growth of investment at high levels.

With reference to the current situation of worldwide stagflation, post-Keynesian economists are in general skeptical that current policies will provide any long-run solution. Government officials in capitalist countries are, for the most part, pursuing restrictive monetary and fiscal policies, often along with "temporary" wage and price controls. The result is that they find themselves doubly cursed with high rates of unemployment and low rates of capacity utilization. Supposedly, a period of prolonged, depressed conditions will convince powerful employer and employee groups that governments are not prepared to guarantee full employment unless these groups moderate their claims for shares of the national output. These measures, by slowing down the current rate of inflation, are then supposed, on the basis of conventional economic analysis, to act so as to whip the inflationary psychology once and for all—that is, reverse people's expectations that prices will continue to rise.

Unfortunately, there is no guarantee that five, ten, or twenty years hence, however long it takes to reverse these expectations (if this can be done at all), double-digit inflation will not resume (in the absence of an incomes policy) when expansionary policies are finally reintroduced in order to curb unemployment. On the contrary, the post-Keynesian view tends to be that these policies are counterproductive in the long run. By substantially reducing growth and creating higher rates of unemployment, the current anti-inflationary policies are seen by most post-Keynesians as creating additional sources of economic, social, and political conflict. These will eventually be reflected in intensified but unrealizable claims by different groups on available output, and these will, in turn, be reflected in a continued cost-push inflationary spiral.

Suppose, then, that it is not possible to whip the inflationary psychology by allowing unemployment rates to remain high for prolonged periods, and that any future attempts to reduce unemployment to more humane levels will be accompanied by a new burst of inflation (again, in the absence of an incomes policy). Suppose, further, it is felt desirable to try to create an economic environment that bears some resemblance to the twenty years of prosperity following World War II. Even here, post-Keynesian macrodynamics has much to say about the structure of a policy that will permit full employment, price stability, and a resumption of growth. Stimulative fiscal and monetary policies, coupled with an incomes policy, will achieve the first two goals. Moreover, the growth goal dictates what form the incomes policy must take. It must be consistent with high levels of investment.

Work by Alfred Eichner (1976) and others has indicated that this requires relatively flexible or unregulated prices insofar as goods and services are concerned. This is not because of a felt need to allow business to raise prices and shift the distribution of income in favor of the capitalist class. The real reason has already been suggested. In large corporations, pricing policy is related to investment policy. When firms need to increase investment outlays and lack the internal funds to do so, they tend to raise prices in order to assure the necessary financing. Flexible product prices allow this important allocative mechanism to work in the interests of economic growth.

What must be controlled are wages. However, in the interests of equity and political acceptability, it is necessary to limit that part of profits that is not retained by corporations for financing investment. This requires policies for taxing dividends and corporate salaries at a rate that keeps the growth of these forms of income in line with the growth of wage income.

None of this is meant to imply that it will be easy to structure an incomes policy consistent with a return to even moderate rates of growth. The actual postwar record of incomes policies in various countries clearly indicates that there are innumerable difficulties. What post-Keynesian economists firmly believe, however, is that before any sensible policy response can be formulated to achieve this or any other desired end, a sound body of theory must be developed that has some explanatory power, that can give policy-makers some insights into the way in which capitalist economies actually evolve over time. And this can only be achieved if there is a sharp and dramatic reorientation of macrodynamic theory away from the neoclassical mode of analysis, back towards its traditional path of intellectual development.

PETER KENYON

Pricing

The microeconomic foundations of post-Keynesian macro-economic theories of growth and distribution have always puzzled critics. They have asserted that, at best, post-Keynesian theory relies on a simple (and unexplained) mark-up pricing formula. The mark-up, however, is merely the most visible element of a quite comprehensive and tightly constructed body of theory that constitutes the microeconomic foundations of post-Keynesian analysis. The mark-up, it turns out, is not only readily explained, it is also the result of a complex set of economic forces operating to produce the growth and distribution observable at the macroeconomic level.

The crux of post-Keynesian theory is the relationship between the savings and investment plans of businessmen. And so it is with the post-Keynesian theory of pricing. In Kaleckian fashion, post-Keynesian theorists divide markets into two broad categories: one, competitive "flexprice" markets in which prices are determined much in the same manner as orthodox theory tells us; and the other, "fixprice" markets in which prices reflect both "normal" production costs (we shall discuss what is meant by "normal" costs below) and the demand for retained profits to finance planned investment expenditures.

The flexprice markets are mainly those concerned with the trading of raw materials and primary foodstuffs. In these markets, a supply of a commodity is delivered to the market and, depending upon the strength of buyers' demands, a price is arrived at which will clear the market for that particular commodity during that market period. For these commodities, supply is more or less fixed during the specified market period.

However, there is another type of commodity for which the conditions of supply are somewhat different. It is the commodity produced by means of other commodities—that is, manufactured or "finished" goods. The production of these goods is quite responsive to variations in demand because there exist (planned) reserves of productive capacity. Therefore, whereas in flexprice markets price adjusts depending on the level of buyers' demand, in fixprice markets changes in demand are met mainly by a change in the volume of output with prices tending to remain relatively unaffected. As John Hicks (1974) has said, in these markets "...we suspend the rule that price must change whenever there is an excess of supply or excess of demand."

Post-Keynesian theorists argue that it is the second type of market which is by far the more important part of the private-enterprise sector of modern capitalist economies. They hold that industries within this sector are largely oligopolistic in structure and that constituent firms, by means of their market power and the conditions of supply for their products, are able to set prices so as to generate sufficient retained profits from expected sales to be able to finance their planned investment expenditure.

The usual approach to oligopoly theory is to regard the mutual interdependence of oligopolistic firms as a static problem: the constituent firms attempt to set prices and quantity targets in order to maximize (individual) profits, but are prevented from finding any one price to achieve this goal, due to uncertainty about their rivals' likely reactions. To get around this difficulty the theorist usually introduces some arbitrary assumption about the probable response of the firms in the industry to the actions of their rivals so that it is possible to arrive at some definitive solution to the problem of how prices are determined. However, it has long been recognized that this line of argument is far from satisfactory, and that oligopoly, the market structure empirically most relevant to an analysis of modern capitalism, stands as an embarrassment to the explanatory power of orthodox economics. As Martin Shubik, in a recent survey of orthodox microeconomics (1970), candidly admitted, "there is no oligopoly theory. . . ." Shubik went on to say that in discussions of oligopoly, "the problems of dynamics appear in their starkest form." This is because, in analyzing oligopolistic behavior, economists have concentrated on price and quantity variables. Yet there is no *a priori* reason why these variables should be selected as the strategic ones. The choice simply reflects the confused concept of competition held by most orthodox economists.

The meaning of competition

In neoclassical theory, competition is viewed both as the process by which a market clearing price is reached through the interaction of demand and supply *and* as a description of a market structure. Indeed competition, as the opposite of monopoly, is considered the type of market structure in which, under stringent assumptions, resources are allocated in a socially optimal manner. The *process* and the *end-state* are thus confused, so that when economists turn to imperfectly competitive situations, they attempt to examine the end-state, the degree of deviation from optimal allocation, without looking at the process by which that end-state has been achieved. Rather, they assume that the process is implicit in the structure. The end-state chosen for examination, namely the resulting resource allocation, is of course arbitrary, but it does make the price variable a logical point of concern.

The attention given to price as the key variable is therefore in keeping with the Walrasian tradition in modern economics, which focuses on allocation rather than on production. This emphasis reflects the neoclassical view of what economics is all about—to wit, the optimal allocation of scarce resources among competing ends. It is understandable, then, as Paul J. McNulty (1968) has observed, that ". . . the emergence of the idea of competition as itself a market structure was a distinguishing contribution of neoclassical economics."

An alternative view of competition is put forth in the classical and Marxian theory. Here rivalry is such as to force the expected rate of profits on new investment to tend towards uniformity between firms and industries. Competition in classical economic thought from Adam Smith to Karl Marx is thus a process, not an end-state. As reflected in investment and growth policies, competition involves the process by which resources are allocated—and, ultimately, income distributed—between social classes over time rather than just their allocation among individuals at a *point* in time. This emphasis reflects the preoccupation of the classical economists (particularly Ricardo and Marx) with the concept of capital and the process of capital accumulation.

If this essentially dynamic, classical view of the competitive process is adopted, rivalry between the constituent firms in an industry need only be sufficient to ensure that no profitable investment opportunities are forgone. The key strategic variable becomes the level of capital expenditures derived from the investment plans of firms, with competitive rivalry focused on relative growth rates and relative market shares. Rather than making short-run profit maximization an end in itself, firms see profits as a means to an end, that of enabling them to expand over time, preferably by increasing their market share. Post-Keynesian writers argue that the behavioral goal of firms is to maximize the growth in sales revenue over time, subject to a minimum profit constraint. (Industrial economists have found, of course, that it is hard to distinguish empirically between growth measured in terms of sales revenue and growth measured in some other manner—for example, in terms of profits over time. But however measured, it is clearly growth that is the goal of the firm.) Again we see the return to classical modes of analysis, with their emphasis on accumulation and on competition among firms as the driving force behind that accumulation.

An important corollary of this approach is that it leads directly to a method of analysis called "periodization," whereby, in the tradition of classical political economy, attention is directed to "causal" links. In other words, certain "effects" (such as the way in which prices and investments are determined) in one time period, can be explained by antecedent "causes" in an earlier time period. This view can be contrasted with the methodological approach of neoclassical economics, in which all factors are deemed to influence each other simultaneously.

The mark-up

The emphasis on "causal" links, with its implicit "periodization," carries over to the post-Keynesian analysis of pricing. Post-Keynesian economists argue that the pricing behavior of oligopolistic firms in the manufacturing sector of industrialized capitalist economies can be explained by the demand for funds from internal sources for purposes of investment expenditure.

The evidence shows that between 75 percent and 90 percent of gross fixed capital expenditures in U.S. manufacturing industry is financed from retained profits (Eichner, 1976). Post-Keynesians conclude, therefore, that oligopolistic firms, having some degree of discretionary power, set their margins above normal production costs, so that they can generate sufficient cash flow to finance from internal sources much of the investment expenditure they wish to undertake. That is, movements in prices depend upon the requirements of firms for internally generated investment funds *and* upon movements in normal production costs. The mark-up is linked directly with the need to finance planned investment expenditure.

The mark-up, according to this view, is arrived at in the following manner. First, the firm (which can be regarded as being the industry price leader for the current pricing period) makes a decision about its future investment plans, based on the relation between the observed rate of capacity utilization and some desired rate of utilization. Desired plant capacity will be such that the firm will be able to meet a sudden increase in demand for its output. Where firms are engaged in battles over market shares under conditions of uncertainty, they will not wish to be caught without the extra capacity needed to accommodate unexpected increases in orders. Investment plans will be based upon the firm's projections as to the future growth of market demand and the estimated profitability of various alternative investment projects.

The firm will then choose a mark-up that will yield the required level of retained profits, given its dividend payout ratio of debt to equity (or gearing ratio). The firm then persists with the price arrived at through this planning process as long as demand conditions indicate that productive capacity is adequate, and as long as production costs do not deviate significantly from their normal level. Capacity utilization, therefore, varies with market demand conditions around some average, or standard, level.

These decisions are made with reference to the state of demand that, experience suggests to the firm, is reasonable. That is to say, the mark-up policy of the firm is influenced by the general state of business confidence. This same state of confidence also determines the firm's investment plans. Investment plans and the size of the mark-up are inexorably linked through the demand and supply of funds in the form of the retained profits with which the firm finances proposed investment projects. Thus actual prices do not reflect current demand conditions; rather they reflect the funds requirements for the planned investment expenditure the firm considers necessary if it is to adjust its capacity sufficiently to meet expected future demand.

This whole conception of pricing is fully in the tradition of classical political economy in which prices are basically production-determined rather than demand-determined. In classical analysis, "natural" prices reflect production costs, with the result that fluctuations in demand do not play any direct role in price determination. The role of demand is not to cause prices to adjust in a thermostatic manner so as to clear markets and achieve the famous Walrasian equilibrium. Rather its role is to shift resources among industries over the longer period through its effects on expected profitability and so on investment. Where expected profit rates are not uniform as between industries (and market prices diverge from "natural" prices), capitalists can be expected to shift resources away from less profitable uses toward more profitable ones. The process of competition takes place through investment and capital accumulation.

Normal costs

The second major determinant of prices, according to post-Keynesian economics, is the level of normal costs. These are defined as the costs which would apply at some standard, or expected, rate of capacity utilization if the economy were on its secular (or long-run) growth path. (Wynne Godley and William Nordhaus (1972) have approximated this empirically with their trend line of the growth in output.) Neither temporary changes in production costs nor temporary changes in product demand directly influence output price to any significant extent. In Keynesian-Kaleckian fashion the level of demand determines the level of economic activity as measured by GNP. It is the level of output and not price which fluctuates with the level of demand over the trade cycle. As Luigi Pasinetti (1974) argues, "The basic feature remains, by contrast with more primitive societies, that [among the factors operating to determine prices] fluctuations of demand have become *unimportant*. Therefore, the traditional response mechanism of price changes having become inoperative, another mechanism is brought into use. To changes in demand, producers respond by changing production."

When expected rates of profits on new investment differ sufficiently to indicate permanent changes in demand, thereby necessitating a shift of resources among industries, investment plans will be formed and profit margins adjusted so that the necessary retained profits can be generated. Both Ricardo and Marx saw profits as the source of accumulation. However, as Adrian Wood (1975) has pointed out, such an explanation of pricing ". . . has never formed part of the mainstream orthodoxy of economics. But closely related ideas have surfaced from time to time."

These related ideas began with the pioneering work of Hall and Hitch (1939) in the late 1930s. Ever since then, empirical studies of pricing behavior, mainly in the manufacturing sectors of modern capitalist economies, have time and again verified mark-up pricing behavior. However, explanations of price behavior based on the cost of production have not been generally accepted by orthodox economists—despite the impeccable classical pedigree of such theories. The reason most generally given has been the lack of an acceptable answer—different from the one given by orthodox economists—to the question: What determines the size of the mark-up? Post-Keynesian economists argue that their approach to price theory provides an answer to that question.

The recent developments in post-Keynesian microeconomics are intuitively appealing. They offer a helpful framework within which the actual behavior of firms and industries in modern capitalist economies may be analyzed, by making what would appear to be realistic assumptions: they take into account differences in pricing behavior between sectors due to differences in the nature of firms' production techniques, and therefore in cost conditions; they explicitly recognize sales revenue maximization over time as the primary objective of firms in the oligopolistic sector; and they recognize the existence of imperfect capital markets—because of imperfect knowledge and uncertainty. The fact that investment expenditure is the centerpiece of the analysis makes the theory explicitly dynamic. The theory, moreover, explains why profits, as a source of investment funds, must necessarily be earned by large industrial corporations.

Indeed, the theory may explain the uncertain findings of industrial economists on the relative profitability of owner-controlled and management-controlled firms. If large oligopolistic firms set profit margins on the basis of expected investment expenditure, the separation of ownership from control may make little difference to the relative performance of firms controlled by management and those controlled by owners. We would expect firms in competitive industries to perform differently from those in the oligopolistic sector, something which empirical evidence does confirm. However, differences in performance *within* the oligopolistic sector may have little to do with the degree of managerial control. Rather, such differences may be explained by variations in pricing behavior and, particularly, by whether or not firms within the oligopolistic sector set their prices in the manner suggested by post-Keynesian writers.

Policy implications

What are some of the policy implications of the post-Keynesian approach to price determination? First, it should be evident from this and the other essays in this volume, that post-Keynesian theory stresses the importance of the level and distribution of income, rather than of reactions to changes in price (substitution possibilities) within the economy. Second, efforts by governments to change the distribution of income have usually been inhibited by an imperfect understanding of the causal relationship between profits and investment and so, by fears of the effects of redistributive policies on employment, productivity, and growth.

Post-Keynesian analysis spells out clearly the relationship among prices, profits, and investment and by so doing, offers considerable insight into the current coincidence of high levels of unemployment and high rates of inflation which beset most industrialized capitalist economies.

Traditional demand management policies which affect the level of activity, and thus the level of unemployment, have very little effect on prices in the oligopolistic sector. As we have seen, it is output and not price which adjusts to changes in the level of aggregate demand—although actual profit margins may be squeezed due to the presence of overhead costs.

If efforts are made to change the functional share of corporate income going either to workers or to capitalists (in the form of either dividends or retained profits), a wage-price spiral will occur. Since changes in the level of income necessarily involve changes in its distribution, such a wage-price spiral is the likely result of demand management policies. Functional shares can be altered in the short period without untoward effect only by securing a change in capitalists' discretionary expenditures (either on consumption or on investment goods). In terms of the post-Keynesian model discussed above, this involves a change in the mark-up. In this sense, capitalists are, in Michal Kalecki's words, "masters of their fate." (Kalecki, 1971).

In negotiations on money wages between workers and capitalists, unions may have their eye on their "fair" or historic share of the total pie. If, therefore, employers have the ability to increase mark-ups as a result of the need to finance investment expenditure, real wages will be eroded as prices rise. Unions may then press for a larger money wage to maintain their "fair" share, and the basis for a wage-price spiral will have been laid. It is for this reason that post-Keynesian economists see a prices and incomes policy as a necessary adjunct to traditional demand-management policies, together with some social mechanism (for example, indicative planning together with selective public sector spending) to direct the amount and type of investment. This is a policy which Keynes (1936) foresaw long ago when he wrote: "I expect to see the State, which is in a position to calculate the marginal efficiency of capital on long views and on the basis of the general social advantage, taking an even greater responsibility for directly organising investment."

Such a policy would open the way for what Joan Robinson in a talk given at Adelaide University in 1976, called "a real social contract which would satisfy the reasonable demands of the workers for more control over their work, more security against redundancy, better social services. . . ." (Harcourt, 1977). That is, the policy would allow wage earners to be more moderate in their money wage demands, secure in the knowledge that the real value of the social wage was being maintained or increased in line with productivity growth (and, of course, exchange rate stability).

* * * *

By way of an epilogue, it should be stressed that the preceding outline of the post-Keynesian approach to price determination is not meant to imply that post-Keynesian economists consider their approach to apply across all markets. Where supply conditions are such that output cannot readily adjust without signficant changes in marginal costs, the whole structure of traditional price theory is obviously relevant. The foregoing discussion did not deal with these markets (which, incidentally, include many, if not most, retail markets), since the aim was to introduce readers to what post-Keynesian economists have to say about price determination in the oligopolistic sector of modern industrialized economies. Post-Keynesian theory is only in an embryonic stage of development, and care must be taken not to claim too much for it.

J. A. KREGEL

Income Distribution

The post-Keynesian approach to income distribution takes
the central proposition of Keynes' theory of output and employment as its point of departure. This proposition can be
summarized briefly in the statement that "given the psychology of the public, the level of output and employment as a
whole depends on the amount of investment." (Keynes, 1936.)
However, the post-Keynesians extend Keynes' theory to argue
that investment is a primary determinant, not only of output
and employment, but also of the distribution of the national
income between wages and profits.

It is, of course, well known that Keynes did not deal explicitly with the question of distribution in *The General
Theory*. Yet, he made a number of suggestions about the effects of the distribution of income on the level of employment and, in particular, on the level and composition of aggregate demand. In addition, Keynes assumed diminishing returns
in his analysis. With a fixed stock of productive capacity, this
implied that prices would be higher when output was higher,
leading to an inverse relation between the level of employment and the purchasing power of an unchanged money wage
rate. Such a relation also implied an inverse relation between
effective demand, output, and employment on the one hand
and the share of wages in total output on the other. But these
implicit relations were never worked out or explored in a for-

mal way.

Thus, when Keynes' pupils and followers, such as Joan Robinson, Richard Kahn, and Nicholas Kaldor, went on to investigate the wider theoretical implications of Keynes' theory of employment (a task which had been postponed by the outbreak of the war), it was perhaps natural that they should attempt to determine, in a more systematic manner, the implications of Keynes' theory of income determination for the analysis of income distribution. This was carried out, however, as part of a more general analysis of the long-term growth of output, a subject which had been the central concern of the classical economists and which Harrod (1939) had reintroduced just prior to World War II.

In this endeavor, it seemed logical for Keynes' followers to construct their arguments about the distribution of aggregate national income on the distinction between wages and profits, that is, in terms of the economic aggregates that Keynes proposed in *The General Theory*. The post-Keynesian theory is thus primarily what is today called "macroeconomic," rather than "microeconomic" (although the original formulation did not recognize such a clear-cut division). Major emphasis is placed on the distribution of aggregate national output between consumption and investment, as the counterpart on the product side to the distribution of income between wages and profits on the income side, with aggregate output itself determined by the relative balance between savings and investment and by the multiplier.

Orthodox theory

In orthodox theory, on the other hand, the distribution of income is determined by the price at which each individual can sell, in the competitive market, the services of the factor of production which he possesses. This approach is primarily concerned with the individual, or personal, distribution of income as determined on the microeconomic level by economic factors trading in specific factor markets. The orthodox theory leads to the following conclusions: (a) that, assuming initial factor endowments are equal, if the supplies of factor services can adjust to the differences in relative factor prices, then personal incomes will be equal; (b) that if there are imperfections in the market mechanism (such as the types of supply limitations imposed by the American Medical Association), or if there are significant differences in innate skills or qualities, then personal incomes will be unequal. Thus, with ability distributed randomly across the population, income will also be random, or statistically normally distributed, that is, the distribution will be bell-shaped.

This approach has often been criticized for its failure to consider institutional, social, and historical factors (though some economists consider this as proof of its general or "scientific" character). There is, however, an even more basic criticism that lies behind the post-Keynesian attempt to construct a more coherent theory of distribution, and this has to do with the basic analytical structure of the neoclassical approach. The orthodox explanation of the distribution of income, in its various forms, is based on the notion of supply and demand operating in competitive markets. The demand for a factor's services is seen as ultimately deriving from the factor's contribution to output at the margin of production —that is, from what is called its "marginal productivity." Profit maximization then requires that no organizer of production pay for the services of a factor more than the use of that factor in the production process will contribute to his receipts from selling the additional output it enables him to produce. In other words, the price of the factor service, and thus the income it receives, should be equal to the value of its marginal product.

The supply of any factor service is, on the other hand, determined by the sacrifice, or disutility, associated with its use.

In the case of labor, this may be viewed as the physical or mental anguish associated with work and, in the case of other factors, with the opportunity cost arising from the forgone income from some alternative use. In a competitive market, where those who control the factors of production are attempting to maximize their well-being, the factor services will be supplied only up to the point where the disutility of an additional unit of service supplied is equal to the increment in income received as a result. That is, the price of the factor service (the income the owner receives) must just offset the marginal disutility of supplying the service.

There are thus two relations, one between price and the quantity of a factor service demanded (the demand function), and the other between the price and the quantity supplied (the supply function). Where the two curves graphing these functional relationships intersect, demand and supply are equal. They represent the determinants of the equilibrium price and quantity sold in competitive markets. It is on the basis of price and quantity that the income received by each factor of production is fixed.

This theory, which relies on equilibrium prices, based on demand and supply, as determined by the marginal productivity and the marginal disutility of various factor services, has been subjected to two different types of criticisms. First, as should now be well known, Keynes (1936) denied that, in the case of labor services, the wage would necessarily be equal to the marginal disutility of the effort being put forward. That is, he disputed that labor could choose the real wage at which it would be employed. Keynes went on to construct a theory to explain the level of employment on quite a different basis—and in the process, he also implicitly denied, as Sidney Weintraub (1956) pointed out long ago, that the demand for labor depends on its marginal productivity. Thus Keynes rejected the notion that either the income of labor or the amount of employment could be determined by marginalist principles operating at the microeconomic level in the labor market. He also rejected the analogous arguments about the income and amount of capital employed, but his reasoning on this point was less explicit.

The second criticism of the orthodox marginalist theory of distribution stems from Piero Sraffa's elaboration (1960) of the classical concept of prices of production. (A similar line of criticism is found in the work of Joan Robinson (1953, 1956), but is based on a somewhat different analytical framework.) Sraffa was able to show, first, that a system of equilibrium prices could be derived independently of any "marginal" changes and, indeed, without direct recognition of the role played by the demand for factor services. In other words, there was no need to rely on the concepts of either marginal productivity or marginal disutility to determine equilibrium prices.

Sraffa was also able to show that, once "capital" services are recognized as deriving from heterogeneous commodities which, instead of passing into the hands of final consumers, are used in the production process, there is no way to measure the "quantity" of capital—except by calculating these "quantities" in value terms. Such values, however, will depend on prices (since the value of any stock of goods is equal to the price times the quantity), and the prices, in turn, will depend on the distribution of income (since, with a different distribution of income, the rate of profit that must be included to cover the services of capital goods in the prices obtained by capital goods will be different). With capital measured in value terms, then the quantity of any stock of capital goods cannot be determined independently of their price. What this means is that no simple monotonic relation can be established between the quantity of capital and its price. This result encompasses the arguments which Joan Robinson (1953) originally put forward against the use of an "aggregate production function"—that is, an equation specifying the quantitative relation between various aggregate inputs, "capital" and labor, and aggregate output—in order to explain the distribution of income. Robinson's criticisms focused on the validity of combining the heterogeneous commodities that constitute the stock of capital goods into a single aggregate measure labeled "capital" which is, at the same time, independent of the particular rate of interest or "price" being used to determine those capital values. For unless this can be done, the valuation placed on the capital stock is not independent of the distribution of income which the "quantity" of capital, after being incorporated in an aggregate production function, is meant to explain. But the criticism that derives from Sraffa's work is, as Pierangelo Garegnani (1960, 1966, 1970) has stressed, more fundamental. For it denies the very logical foundations of a demand curve based on marginal productivity (not only for capital, but for all factor services), and thus it vitiates the explanation of the distribution of income based, as the orthodox explanation is, on the determination of prices for factor services, through the market, as a reflection of supply and demand conditions. This criticism is obviously more powerful in its generality than the criticism arising from the difficulty of calculating a value aggregate for capital which can then be used in a production function.

Keynes and Kalecki

In light of these two lines of criticism directed at the orthodox theory, one derived from Keynes' analysis, the other from Sraffa's, the post-Keynesians attempt to build a coherent theory of distribution on the earlier work of the classical economists, together with the modern approach to explaining aggregate output and employment. In this endeavor, there are two basic starting points. The first is Keynes' own *Treatise on Money*, in which the analysis of the distribution of income figured more prominently than in *The General Theory*. Second, and perhaps more important, is the work of the Polish economist, Michal Kalecki (1966). Kalecki had developed an explanation for the determination of the level of employment at about the same time as Keynes, but Kalecki's approach was based more directly on the relationship of investment and prices to income distribution. Kalecki's version of the theory has been summed up in the adage that "the workers spend what they get; the capitalists get what they spend." The point can be most simply demonstrated by reference to the national income and product (expenditure) accounts.

National income, as is well known, can be measured in two ways, namely from the side of income and from the side of expenditures, as follows:

Income	*Expenditure*
Profits (Income of Capitalists)	Investment
+ Wages (Income of Workers)	+ Capitalists' Consumption
	+ Workers' Consumption
= National Income	= National Product

Following Kalecki, the national income can be divided into the profits received by the capitalists and the wages received by the workers. The national product, on the other hand, can be divided into investment and the consumption by the capitalists and the consumption by the workers. Investment includes the purchase of fixed capital (machinery, buildings, etc.) and any change in inventories.

With the workers assumed to spend all their earnings on consumption, the wages they receive as income must necessarily be equal to the value of workers' consumption goods produced since all their income is spent on them. This means that the income of the capitalists, profits, will be equal to the value of the goods purchased by the capitalists with their profits, both for investment and for consumption. Two striking conclusions emerge from this simple classification of the economic system. The first is that the capitalists can increase the share of national income they receive as profits simply by increasing the amount they spend on investment, with the higher level of investment leading, of course, to an increase in aggregate output based on the multiplier. On the other hand, even if the capitalists consume their profits in high living rather than investing, they do not suffer a reduction in their profit income. As far as the capitalists' income is concerned, it is maintained independently of how it is spent—or, as Keynes described the situation (1930), capitalists' profits are like the widow's cruse which cannot be emptied no matter how much is taken out of it.

The modern post-Keynesian approach

These simple relations form the core of the modern, post-Keynesian approach to income distribution which emphasizes:

1. The control of investment, and thus growth, by profit recipients (either entrepreneurs or large corporations) and the control of prices by producers (oligopolistic corporations).

2. The dependence of the rate of change of output per worker on the rate of gross investment and technical progress.

3. An interdependence between the growth of output on the one hand and the distribution of income between wages and profits on the other hand (with that interdependence affecting the willingness and ability of entrepreneurial organizations to carry out investment).

In the development of these points, post-Keynesian theory uses the same classification of economic aggregates as Keynes in *The General Theory*. The exposition of this approach can be simplified, and at the same time its link to classical theory demonstrated, by invoking two assumptions about the propensity to consume out of different types of incomes. The two assumptions already encountered in connection with

J. A. Kregel

Kalecki's work, are that:

1. All wages are spent on consumption (wage or necessary) goods. This is the modern-day equivalent of assuming a subsistence wage. It gives rise to a consumption function for which consumer expenditures, given the money wage, are a function of the level of employment.

2. All profits are used to purchase new investment goods. This corresponds to the case of the idealized classical entrepreneur who ploughs back his profits to expand the family business; and it gives rise to an investment demand function in which investment (and saving) is equal to earned profits.

If the analysis is further simplified by aggregating output into the categories, consumption goods and investment goods —with each type produced in an identifiably different sector of the economy—it is possible to examine the flow of goods and of incomes between the two sectors. To bring out the salient points, it is customary to assume, as did Keynes, that the level of investment is determined exogenously. Keynes himself (1936) used the catch phrase "animal spirits" to indicate that decisions to invest were based on a more complex set of factors than just accrued profits or the availability of finance. To make the analysis tractable it is also necessary to assume a "given psychology of the public" and given technical conditions.

Under these simple assumptions, the amount of investment and the ruling technology determine the level of employment and the division of labor between the production of wage goods and the production of investment goods. The technical conditions and existing capacity also then determine the total output of each type of good. Thus there is a determinate quantity of wage goods that will meet the flow of spending as determined by workers' incomes, and a determinate quantity of investment goods produced in response to the entrepreneurs' expectation of future earnings from combining them with labor to produce output. Realized profits on the production of wage goods and investment goods will depend on the relation of prices to prime, or direct, costs of production (for simplicity, wage costs are assumed to be the sole prime costs). In the wage good sector, demand is equal to the wage bill in both the consumption and investment sectors, and as a result, its receipts will exceed its wage costs by an amount equal to the wage bill in the investment sector. This provides funds for the purchase of investment goods by the wage good sector.

Producers in the investment goods sector will also demand investment goods for their own use. The sales of this sector to firms in the wage good sector must cover the labor costs of production so that any and all additional investment goods produced for its own use represent the excess of sales over costs—that is, they are equal to the profits in the investment goods sector.

The profits of both sectors combined must then be equal to the value of the net investment goods produced while the real value of wages (money wages adjusted by the price of wage goods) must be equal to the amount of wage goods produced. This is because only the profits of both sectors combined are available to purchase the output of the investment goods sector, and only the wages earned in both sectors are available to purchase the output of the wage good sector. Here the distribution of income between wages and profits is mirrored by the division of national output between wage goods and investment goods (and, given the technology, by the division of labor between the investment and wage good sectors). A higher proportion of investment in total output, causing employment in the investment sector to be higher relative to that in the wage good sector, then leads to a higher share of profits relative to wages in national income, and vice versa. This is, of course, the same basic relation demonstrated above in terms of the national income accounts.

The discussion thus far owes more to Keynes than to

J. A. Kregel

Kalecki, since it starts with investment and goes through employment and prices to distribution. Kalecki, on the other hand, initiated his investigation by recognizing the ability of firms to determine the margin of prices over cost, reflecting the "degree of monopoly." Given the firms' decisions on the level of prices relative to average prime costs, the equilibrium level of employment and the level of expected profits would both be determined with the latter triggering the investment decisions by firms that would, in turn, determine the division of national income between wages and profits.

As indicated above, the post-Keynesian approach takes into account both these factors—the influence of investment on prices (Keynes) and the influence of prices on investment (Kalecki). For not only do firms have the ability to determine their investment plans (the aggregate of these individual decisions concerning investment determining the aggregate level of investment epending), they also have the ability to determine the prices at which they will sell their output (which, when combined with the level of demand as determined by the aggregate level of investment and consumption, determines the quantity sold at these prices and thus, given costs, their profits). Much of the recent post-Keynesian literature has been concerned with the investigation of the relation between the setting of prices on current output and the decisions about future productive capacity, along with the effect these two decisions have on the determination of the shares of wages and profits in national income.

Workers' savings

In the early stages of the development of the post-Keynesian approach to income distribution, it was believed by some economists that the results were highly dependent on the simplifying assumptions noted above, especially those concerning consumption out of various types of incomes. It was easy to see that consumption out of profits caused no particular problems for, *ceteris paribus*, this would merely cause the demand for wage goods (in this case, because of the greater demand for wage goods coming from profit recipients) to be higher relative to the supply, thereby giving rise to proportionately higher prices and profits, and proportionately lower wages. This is precisely the case of the widow's cruse described above. In such a situation, profits would exceed investment in the same proportion as the profits are used to purchase consumption (wage) goods. The case of saving out of workers' wages, however, did not seem so straightforward.

Savings by workers have the opposite effect on the share of wage goods in aggregate output. They reduce the expenditure on wage goods relative to the expenditure on investment goods and thus, over time, lead to a fall in the relative price of wage goods, an increase in the purchasing power of workers, and a rise in the real wage. Allowing for savings out of wages produces an additional complication, for if workers are saving, it must be for some purpose—to purchase income-producing financial assets, for example. They must then share, indirectly or directly, in aggregate profits, in terms of interest or dividends received. Workers would thus receive combined incomes composed of both wages and profits so that the real value of the money wage must be distinguished clearly from the real value of the workers' combined incomes. However, as Luigi Pasinetti (1962) has shown, as long as the analysis is limited to the distribution of income between wages and profits as categories of income, the existence of savings out of wages makes no difference to the results. The savings behavior of workers does, however, influence the share of their aggregate combined incomes (in terms of the proportion of total profits they receive as interest or dividends) in the total national income.

Despite this result, some economists still believed the theory to be dependent on the existence of historically definable classes of wage and profit recipients, or that it was limited by viewing distribution in these "class-based" terms. Irrespective of the merit that most political economists attach to an analysis related to social classes, Pasinetti's approach, when taken to its logical limits, can provide the basis for an analysis of personal distribution as well. Once wage earners also receive some nonwage income, say interest on savings, rents, or profits, they must be grouped according to some criterion other than their income source—in terms of their asset preferences, for example. The number of different "classes" could, in the limiting case, coincide with the number of individual income recipients. Indeed, Pasinetti's original intention was to extend the theory to many income classes. However, no matter how many such classes are considered, or how they are determined, his basic result concerning the irrelevance of saving out of wages for the distribution of income between the income categories of wages and profits (but not amongst the variously defined other social groups) holds as long as there is at least one of these groups that receives only profits income.

Implications of the analysis

The post-Keynesian theory of distribution thus highlights the role of investment, employment, growth, and prices in the division of national income. It contrasts with the orthodox theory by showing that the incomes earned in society can be explained independently of any direct relation to individual or class productivity. From this point of view, it is no longer possible to justify unequal incomes on the basis of differential productivity nor the difference between wages and profits on the same grounds. Income differentials are thus neither natural nor economic facts, but the result of social and political custom and decisions, as well as market power. At the same time, by demonstrating the relations among growth, distribution, and prices (or the mark-up of prices over costs), the theory shows that there will necessarily be strict relations among the rate of growth of the economy, the distribution of income between the saving and nonsaving classes, and the price level. Policies to influence any one of these factors can be expected to have an impact on the other factors simultaneously.

Given the fundamental differences between the post-Keynesian and orthodox explanations for the distribution of income it is quite natural that there should be differences in the policy stances derived from the two positions. As already mentioned, the orthodox justification of income inequality in terms of productivity differences finds no support in the post-Keynesian approach, as was emphasized by Edward Nell in his 1973 paper. Neither can profits be explained in terms of a return to a "productive" factor "capital." This was demonstrated by both Garegnani and Sraffa in 1960. Nor, finally, is inequality required to provide incentives for higher rates of growth as Paul Davidson notes in a 1973 article.

While such a position suggests that there are no economic obstacles to a more equitable distribution of income, it does not imply that profit can be eliminated, nor that income equality can be treated independently of other factors. At the aggregate level, the theory shows that, given the state of technical knowledge, any desired growth rate requires a particular utilization of the economy's resources for investment. The remaining resources are then available to provide for current consumption. At the same time, nominal incomes must be distributed such that total incomes less expenditure on available consumption goods equal the value of aggregate investment. Yet, there is no presumption that any particular distribution of income between wages and profit, or any particular distribution of individual incomes, is necessary to achieve this result.

Finally, it is common for those who operate within a post-Keynesian framework to recommend the use of incomes policies as a means of controlling inflation. This stems from the basic proposition that, for any given rate of growth and associated saving-investment pattern, the level of prices is primarily determined by the level of wages or, more directly, wage costs per unit of output. Thus, given the mark-up of prices over costs, if unit costs can be kept in step with productivity, prices should be relatively stable.

At the same time, the theory shows clearly that such policies also imply a definite distribution of income among the various groups in society. Incomes policies thus affect not only prices, but also the distribution of income. From this perspective, wages policy cannot be justified independently of an investment policy to assure the full utilization of the economy's productive capacity and labor force. These are, of course, not only economic questions concerning the structure and functioning of labor and commodity markets; they are also social and political questions which lie at the heart of political economy. The point of the post-Keynesian approach is that it is no longer sufficient to appeal to the impersonal forces of perfectly competitive markets to justify economic conditions.

A. ASIMAKOPULOS

Tax Incidence

The incidence of taxation has long held a fascination for economists. It has been recognized for some time that the economic incidence of a tax might differ from its legal incidence. For example, François Quesnay, Louis XV's physician at Versailles, who developed the famous Tableau Économique, argued that taxes, no matter where levied, would eventually come out of the agricultural net product (*produit net*), as this was the only surplus income produced by the economy. Today, to give another example, most economists do not believe that the burden of the sharp increases in payroll taxes that have been imposed to cover rising social security costs will be borne by the firms legally obligated to pay these taxes. Instead the higher taxes are likely to be reflected in higher prices for the firms' products. There are, however, important differences among economists about the economic incidence of other taxes. The incidence of the corporate profits tax has been a matter of particular controversy.

These differences are to be found even among proponents of neoclassical economic theory who, in their analyses, assume full employment and then try to deduce the incidence of a profits tax from a microeconomic perspective alone. For example, Harberger, in an influential article on this subject (1962), assumes perfectly competitive markets, with firms trying at all times to maximize profits. The prices at which the firms sell their output and their costs of production are all given independently of the tax. In this situation, the initial burden of a profits tax must fall on the earnings of firms, since they have no scope, under the competitive conditions assumed, for increasing their pre-tax profits. Baumol (1959), on the other hand, has pointed out that if firms operate as restrained monopolists, with sales rather than profits being maximized, or if they operate with a pricing rule that does not maximize short-run profits, then firms may be in a position to pass on higher profits taxes through the mechanism of higher prices.

The post-Keynesian approach to tax incidence differs fundamentally from both variants of neoclassical theory because it does not assume that the macroeconomic effects of a broad-based tax, such as a profits tax, can be ignored. A higher profits tax, even if the government maintains a balanced budget by spending the extra revenue it obtains, would affect aggregate demand and thus alter pre-tax profits. This well-known effect of balanced increases in government tax revenues and expenditures is referred to in the economics literature as the "balanced-budget multiplier." Neoclassical economists have, however, ignored it in their consideration of the incidence of taxation. A balanced increase in tax revenues and government expenditures due, say, to an increase in the profits tax, would be expansionary because the government spends all of the revenues raised through this tax, while those who were taxed would have spent only part of what was taxed away and would have saved the rest. This expansionary effect would exist whether the economy were operating at full employment or at less than full employment, and whether markets were competitive or oligopolistic.

But the consequences of this effect depend, of course, on the nature of markets and the initial state of the economy. For example, if the economy were at full employment and markets were competitive, then the expansionary effect of the balanced increase in the government's budget would result in higher prices, with no change in output and employment. If, on the other hand, the economy were operating at less than full employment and markets were oligopolistic, the expansionary effect would be largely reflected in higher output and employment as firms responded to the increased demand by producing and selling more at their established prices. In both these cases, however, pre-tax profits would change as a result of the change in government taxation and expenditure.

The post-Keynesian view

Post-Keynesian theory has been developed from the writings of John Maynard Keynes and Michal Kalecki, but in the theory of tax incidence the influence of Kalecki is the more important one. After developing his theory of effective demand and his macroeconomic theory of distribution, which pointed to investment and capitalist consumption expenditures as the determinants of profits, he published a path-breaking article on the incidence of taxation in the *Economic Journal* (1937). This article pointed out that if investment expenditures in the current short period can be taken to be predetermined because of the time lags involved in the investment process, and if capitalists' consumption expenditures respond only to actual (rather than to expected) changes in their incomes, then an increase in a profits tax will not lower after-tax profits. This is because these profits are given by the predetermined level of investment expenditures and by the capitalists' consumption. Unfortunately, Kalecki's article did not receive the attention it deserved, and the neoclassical theory of tax incidence was developed without taking his argument into account. It is only in recent years, with the articles by John Eatwell (1971), and A. Asimakopulos and John Burbidge (1974), that Kalecki's approach has been developed into a post-Keynesian theory of tax incidence.

The post-Keynesian approach to the incidence of taxation begins with an examination of conditions in the short period during which a tax rate is changed. Investment is taking place within this short period, but changes in productive capacity can be neglected because the addition to total productive capacity due to the completion of investment projects in one of these intervals of time is usually small relative to the total productive capacity available at the beginning of such a period. This short period can be identified with real calendar time, for example, a quarter of a year, a half a year, or even a year. This period of time is long enough to allow for variations in the rate of output with the given productive capacity; but the time lag between investment decisions and the resulting investment activity is generally greater, so that the rate of investment in each of these short periods can be realistically assumed to be largely predetermined.

Post-Keynesian theory also distinguishes between the propensity to save out of wages and the propensity to save out of profits. For purposes of expository convenience it is often assumed that the propensity to save out of wages is zero (and this convention will be followed in this article), but the crucial assumption is that the propensity to save out of profits is greater than that to save out of wages. This assumption has a very strong empirical foundation because of the modern corporation's proclivity for retaining profits. The propensity to save out of profits is equal to the firms' retention ratio plus the proportion of dividend and interest income saved by capitalists.

An economy (where exports and imports, and the government's budget, are balanced) is said to be in short-period equilibrium when the predetermined investment is realized, and this level of investment is equal to what, given their incomes in this period, the individuals and firms choose to save. This equilibrium condition plus the assumption of no saving out of wages (or more generally, a higher propensity to save out of profits) is sufficient to determine post-tax profits in real terms as a function of the saving propensities and the rate of investment in real terms. If the government announces and implements a higher rate of profits tax at the beginning of the short period, and spends the extra revenue it obtains from this increase, then post-tax profits in this period will be unaffected by the tax if short-period equilibrium is reestablished.

This conclusion holds for competitive as well as for non-competitive market conditions—it does not require firms to use previously unexploited monopoly powers when the profits tax is increased—since government expenditures, even when financed by an equal increase in taxes, have an expansionary effect on the economy. There is, as mentioned previously, a multiplier effect on the economy of balanced increases in government tax revenues and expenditure. The decrease in private expenditures due to the increases in taxes is less than the balancing increases in government expenditures because the tax increase is partially absorbed by a reduction in private saving. If there is unemployment initially, then this multiplier effect will lead to higher output and employment. If markets are competitive, this expansion will be accompanied by lower real-wage rates because the increased demand leads to higher prices relative to wages and hence to costs. The resulting higher pre-tax profits make it possible for post-tax profits to be unchanged, even though the profits-tax rate is higher. If markets are oligopolistic, rather than competitive, the multiplier effect of this government policy will be reflected in a sharper increase in output and employment. The leading firms in these markets set prices by adding mark-ups to standard costs, calculated on assumed rates of output that are less than the full capacity rates. Short-period fluctuations in demand in these markets are reflected largely in changes in the amount of output sold at prices set in this way. These firms' profits can increase substantially with higher demand, even with constant prices, because of the higher sales and the decrease in average costs as fixed costs are spread over larger volume. With this change in the distribution of income in post-Keynesian models, occurring as a result of changes in government fiscal policy, the legal and economic incidence of taxation can differ even when attention is focused only on short-run adjustments.

The neoclassical view

The dominant neoclassical analysis of the incidence of a profits tax, associated with Arnold C. Harberger (1962), is based on a view of the world that differs in important respects from that of the post-Keynesians. The short-run distribution of pre-tax income is assumed to be unaffected by an increase in the profits tax (if government expenditure is increased by an amount equal to this tax revenue) and thus the short-run incidence of a higher profits tax is borne entirely by firms. The macroeconomic model that can be constructed to support Harberger's conclusion, as sketched out by Peter Mieszkowski (1969), can be labeled pre-Keynesian. It assumes that full employment of labor and other factors is automatically achieved through wage and price flexibility, with factor returns being determined by technology and resource endowments, that is, by their marginal productivity. There is no room for an independent investment function in this model. Investment depends on saving; and if it is further assumed that the government spends the tax proceeds from a higher profits tax in the same way they would have been spent by those who pay the tax, then the pre-tax distribution of income is unaffected. The short-period economic incidence of the tax must be the same as the legal incidence. There is no room for the balanced-budget multiplier in Harberger's model; full employment is continuously maintained and government spending out of tax revenues precisely replaces the private spending that is curtailed by the raising of these tax revenues. The post-Keynesian approach is more in keeping with the capitalist economies in the real world, where unemployment continues to exist and the causes of cyclical fluctuations defeat the efforts of policy-makers to eliminate them.

The empirical evidence

Recently there have been several econometric studies of the short-run effects of a profits tax, beginning with the major study by Marian Krzyzaniak and Richard Musgrave (1963). They claimed that their study showed that the manufacturing corporate income tax was completely shifted forward to consumers in the short run, and this statement has resulted in considerable controversy and a whole spate of studies. John Cragg, Harberger, and Mieszkowski responded with their own empirical study in defense of Harberger's theoretical conclusion about the short-run incidence of this tax (1967). They added some cyclical variables to the Krzyzaniak-Musgrave model and they concluded that there is no short-run shifting of the corporate income tax. Burbidge (1976) has examined many of these empirical studies. He shows that they are inconsistent because their theoretical underpinnings combine the pre-Keynesian models where full employment prevails with *ad hoc* cyclical variables that are inserted to handle the cyclical fluctuations which, though they exist in the real world, are denied by their models. The empirical estimates they obtain for the effects of changes in taxes cannot be used to test the neoclassical theory because the equations being fitted are not specified by this theory; they are the result of *ad hoc* empirical work based on some incompletely specified

Keynesian model. These estimates for a world where unemployment exists, and where government tax and expenditure policy affects the level of employment and the distribution of income, cannot shed any light on the effects of tax changes in a fictional neoclassical world where unemployment is impossible and where the pre-tax distribution of income is unaffected by changes in taxes. Once the possibility of cyclical fluctuations is admitted—and even neoclassical economists acknowledge this possibility when faced with the data of an actual economy—then it is necessary to investigate the possible relationship between changes in specific tax rates and changes in aggregate demand, that is, it is necessary to work with a well-developed Keynesian (or Kaleckian, or post-Keynesian) model.

The post-Keynesian approach to the incidence of taxation provides the necessary scope to deal with the real world, but much remains to be done in developing it further. Kalecki's examination of this subject was based solely on the comparison of positions of short-period equilibrium and most of the results reported by Asimakopulos and Burbidge (1974) are also obtained in this way. (Asimakopulos and Burbidge, however, do point out that the struggle over income shares between different groups in the economy may be sparked anew by tax and expenditure changes, and this struggle may lead to inflationary changes in wages and prices that lie outside the models that have been developed to date.) The presence of unintended saving, which will occur if the multiplier effects of the change in the government's fiscal policy are not fully worked out by the end of the period, or the presence of unintended inventory changes which cause planned and actual investment to differ, will affect the results. For example, a higher profits tax imposed to cover higher government expenditures will fall partly on after-tax profits if the multiplier effect of this change has not been completed and the ratio of saving to income is greater than the desired ratio. This delay in the working out of the full expansionary effects of the balanced increase in the government's budget would result in an increase in profits in the initial short period that was less than the increase in the profits tax. If firms responded to this drop in after-tax profits by cutting back on current investment decisions and on investment in future periods, then the economic incidence of this tax increase would be borne partly by the firms. The final effects of the tax changes cannot be determined until their repercussions on investment decisions and investment are known. Unplanned changes in inventories have an effect on post-tax profits similar to disequilibrium saving. Profits will increase initially by less than the rise in taxes if the increased demand due to the balanced-budget multiplier is not fully anticipated by firms, and thus leads to a reduction in inventories rather than an expansion of output equal to the increase in demand. If firms respond by increasing production to rebuild inventories and to meet the higher demand, without changes in their investment plans, then the resulting increase in sales and profits will eventually compensate for the higher profits tax.

The conclusion that a higher profits tax does not affect after-tax profits (when the government spends this tax revenue) therefore requires that the firms' investment plans be realized and that they not be adjusted before the expansionary effects of this tax change are completed. A further step in the development of the post-Keynesian approach should be its extension to cover a sequence of short periods, with investment over this time span being explained by the model. The possible implications of the time lags in the multiplier process could then be examined within the context of this expanded model.

Policy implications

Post-Keynesian theory does not provide a single answer to the question of the economic incidence of taxation; rather, it provides a framework for the examination of this question— a framework that contains essential features of the world in which we live. It makes clear that the incidence of taxation cannot be determined without reference to the wider question of the distribution of income. Here post-Keynesian theory points to the conflict between workers and capitalists over income shares—a conflict whose outcome is more favorable to capitalists if firms can establish high mark-ups and high levels of investment expenditures. Workers try to improve their share by bargaining for higher money-wage rates, but this will only lead to an increase in their real-wage rates and income shares if firms are unable to maintain their mark-ups. Inflation is one of the symptoms of this conflict over income shares, as firms raise prices in an effort to restore their mark-ups on the higher wage costs. Increased government expenditures—even if matched by an increase in taxes—could set off a renewed round of price and wage increases, as the various groups in the economy try to shift to others the burden of the increased taxation.

The tax laws do not by themselves provide information on the economic burden of taxation, and the question of "who pays" can, in the end, be determined only by an appropriate economic theory. The political support for a combined tax-and-expenditure program could very well depend on one's conclusions about the economic incidence of the proposed tax.

RICHARD X. CHASE

Production Theory

As Joseph Schumpeter once pointed out (1954), economic theory is the outgrowth of a "vision," one which orders in the
mind the structure and function of some systemic economic
entity. In this view, economic theory plays a cognitive role
closely akin to that of analogy. That is, theoretical construc-
tion is very largely a process that aims to bring forth some particular envisioned (economic) configuration, in a form that is, in
the first instance, communicable so that it may be, in the second instance, capable of analytical articulation and elaboration. The latter characteristics provide the basis for a continuing research program and for guidance in policy definition
and formulation. Schumpeter, for example, traces Keynes'
vision of an unstable capitalism from his *Economic Consequences of the Peace* in 1919 through to the theoretic idea-
system presented in *The General Theory* of 1936 which was
primarily designed to influence the theoretical perceptions of
a select few, his "fellow economists." (Clearly, Keynesian-type
policy was then widely espoused.)

Because of its nature, economic theory cannot ever be
taken as complete or "true." The only meaningful evaluation
of it turns on its being "not false" and on its being useful in
supporting and directing research and policy endeavors. Thus
when theory-system anomalies or disconfirmations arise, and

when these are sufficiently numerous or important to place accepted economic theory and its related vision in serious doubt, the whole course of the discipline's research and policy-related activities must also come into serious question.

The above brief remarks on an aspect of the metaphysics of economic theory, and therefore of policy, will serve to establish a basic framework for the following sketch of fundamental aspects of a recent theoretical debate: the so-called "capital controversy" and its taproot, the "reswitching" theorem. The aim of this essay will be to bring out some key implications of this argument—implications that have been either underemphasized or lost in the welter of technical detail arising from professional controversy. The purpose will be to place what might seem to be a fairly confined display of economic esoterica into a broader perspective, particularly since the issues are related to the fundamental vision of the economic system and to the basic approaches for managing and directing that system which are an outgrowth of the current orthodoxy of economic theory.

Vision

The easiest way to capture the essence of the orthodox, neoclassical vision of the structure of the enterprise economy is to call to mind the simple but profound picture of the familiar "circular flow" of incomes and outputs, along with its message of an integrated market-price system. This system (1) links together various output markets of goods and services, (2) links together various markets for resource inputs, and (3), in finale, gives overall coherence to the whole by coordinating the output side of the system's flows with the input side.

No one, of course, would argue that the simple circular flow analogy is true; just that it is not false regarding fundamentals and therefore that it is useful. This is to say that despite various market imperfections, frictions, and so forth, basic economic forces that inhere in the real world are captured by and "explained" by this theoretic analogy—most particularly those possessing a general tendency toward systemic integration and order. The important point here is that the market dynamics subsumed in the model—even if temporarily or periodically frustrated, sublimated, not acted on, or not transmitted—do in fact exist; and that, moreover, they operate in consistent fashion to bring about economic coherence and order in production and distribution within the system as a whole.

With the "invention" and development of Keynesianism in all its variants, even such questions as innate tendencies toward "full employment," "stability," and "equilibrium" were no longer crucial to the essence of this vision. These states could be purposively brought about by guiding and manipulating, through aggregative tools, the real-world counterpart of the model. Such an approach is logically tenable as long as the actual systemic entity is in fact tied together by market forces that act in a consistent and coherent fashion, with the economic actors, by and large, responding rationally to the signals they receive through the market. And one thing that is crucial to such rationality and market coordination is the existence of the straightforward and intuitively sensible principle of substitution: that in the marketplace the tendency exists for purchasers to substitute for something that has become (relatively) higher in price, something that is (relatively) lower in price.

What is of central importance at this point is *not* that economic rationality always prevails in the marketplace, but rather that market dynamics show no *systematic* tendencies that would cause economic actors to behave in a perverse manner regarding the principle of the (rational) substitution of the cheaper for the more expensive. For such a perversity would negate the model's central message and vision, that a tendency toward coherence and order in matters economic is inherent in the system.

Anomaly

The coherent ordering of the production or factor-input side of the neoclassical schema depends upon this basic principle of rational substitution among resource inputs, specifically between capital and labor as their relative prices change. For example, a relatively lower real wage should work to produce incentives that will tend to induce more rather than fewer labor-intensive production techniques to be employed and vice versa.

Joan Robinson (1953, 1956) was among the first to point out that substitution within the production process might not always take place along the lines suggested by neoclassical theory—that is, between capital and labor inputs as their relative price varied. Her insight emanated from the notion that "capital"—or rather capital goods—is in actuality heterogeneous and needs to be analyzed as such. Capital goods consist of specific plants, together with the specific equipment needed to produce a specific output. Moreover, equipment must often be used in fixed combination with labor and raw materials. Thus, it is not simply a matter of adding or subtracting "capital" inputs to or from the other inputs used in the production process, as the neoclassical theory would suggest is the case. Indeed, there may be no room for factor substitution in response to changes in factor prices except by "switching" from one fixed-proportion technique to another.

The upshot of Robinson's early analysis was that under such conditions (heterogeneous capital and fixed-factor proportions), there may be times at which the change of technique appears to be perverse. For example, a relative *fall* in the price of capital (say, because of a rise in real wages) could be associated with the selection of a production technique that is of a *lower*, rather than of a higher, capital intensity. The fact that capital goods must themselves be produced, using capital and labor inputs and allowing for a period of gestation, is the main reason for this perverse outcome. A rise in the real wage rate may, because of their more labor-intensive method of production, increase the cost of capital goods relative to the cost of labor. In short, the principle of substitutability may be at work, but it may operate in a way opposite to that suggested by the orthodox neoclassical theory.

Robinson's observation, however, was seen at first largely as a technical problem in capital production theory (1956). And indeed even she treated it as a "curiosum," almost whimsically labeling it "the Ruth Cohen Case" ("a private joke," she wrote). Also, as she herself notes, the clue leading to her investigation of this curiosity came from Piero Sraffa's "Preface" to Ricardo's *Principles*, and it was not until 1960 with the publication of Sraffa's *Production of Commodities by Means of Commodities* that the import of the phenomenon came to be more widely recognized. For Sraffa's treatment showed that the perverse changes in production techniques, now known as "reswitching," were of broader theoretical scope and importance than had originally been perceived. This transformed what was seen largely as a technical curiosity into a theoretical anomaly of major proportions, one having profound implications, not only for the validity of neoclassical theories of capital and production, but also for the validity of the neoclassical vision itself.

The perception of this threat is what led to the now famous "capital controversy" of the 1960s between Cambridge on the Charles, USA and Cambridge on the Cam, UK. Because of its import, an examination of Sraffa's generalization of the reswitching phenomenon is in order.

Richard X. Chase

Anomaly extended: theoretical crisis

Broadly put, reswitching (or double-switching as it is sometimes called) relates to economic incentives that favor a *particular* production technique, or capital-labor ratio, *at more
than one level of relative factor prices*, with other techniques
being desirable at intermediate levels. A useful example of
this, originally alluded to by Sraffa, is wine-making, where
capital intensity is relatively low in the very beginning of the
production process (picking and sorting), but very high for
the remainder of the process as the wine is held to maturity
(via capital goods)—five years, it seems, being a minimum
period for a merely palatable wine. (Sraffa contrasts this instance to the "old oak made into the chest" situation where
the reverse labor-capital intensity is the case, in that cutting
and processing timber is more capital-intensive than the subsequent carpentering and finishing.)

In wine-making, an increase in the rate of interest would
have strong effects on the costs of production, particularly
felt through the highly capital-intensive aging phase of the
process. Thus an increase in interest costs would probably
tend to induce producers to economize by shortening the
aging stage closer to its limits, given the acceptable quality
standards for the wine. Such a "switch," of course, would
tend to lower the capital intensity of the process as a whole
(conversely raising its labor intensity), and would be in
accord with what neoclassical theory would predict in light
of the increase in interest costs. However, further increases in
the rate of interest would, at a point, raise the costs of holding
wine so much that producers would find it advantageous to
switch to some technique of higher capital intensity that
would speed up, that is, shorten, the production process. The
latter switch would be perverse according to orthodox theory
and its "law" of substitution—this, of course, calling for
higher labor intensity and lesser capital intensity as the cost
of capital rises. But how does one transform what is largely a

parable of assertions into a parable of significant and general economic importance?

The key to the transformation noted above lies with time and the resulting *compounding effects* of interest rate changes on the comparative cost of the capital and labor inputs. For example, the compounded effects of an interest rate increase on such long-term processes as wine-producing would be quite significant, particularly when capital intensity becomes quite high early in the production process (when the aging stage commences). Thus, as interest costs rise, it may pay at first to cut capital intensity by, say, cutting the term of the aging stage; but if interest costs rise further, the exponential compounding of interest charges will give rise to a situation where it will pay to switch and to use *more* capital—particularly if applied toward the end of the production process where the results of compounding will be relatively slight—so as to shorten the time required in the process of production. Thus, the switching of technique back to a more capital-intensive method can also have the effect of changing the types of capital used in production. And so it is not merely the degree of capital intensity that is altered, but also what form "capital" takes in the production process and thus the duration and very nature of that process itself. The foregoing factors are of importance since they affect the time period over which compounding takes place, and thus the points of desirable switching and reswitching. And this is the cutting edge: in light of the foregoing argument, it can reasonably be expected that changes in the relative costs of labor and capital—real wages and interest or profit rates—will work to induce *rational* substitutions of capital for labor, and labor for capital, that lack the consistency and ordered coherence postulated by neoclassical capital and production theory. Such a situation, of course, would also strike at the very essence of the neoclassical vision of how production is ordered or coordinated in a market system.

The upshot of this controversy was a flurry of esoteric

debate and fulmination primarily centering around the two Cambridges of economics fame. By the mid-1960s, not only did the existence and relevance of the anomaly carry the field when the proponents of Cambridge USA acknowledged that reswitching, and therefore the Cambridge UK criticism of neoclassical theory, was indeed valid, but also the even stronger point was brought to light that, although reswitching is a sufficient condition, it is not even a necessary one for indeterminacy in neoclassical production functions. Work by John Hicks (1965) and others has shown that it is a simple technological fact of economic life that, with heterogeneous capital goods and fixed-factor techniques, there exist wide areas where production is so structured that orthodox neoclassical relations between the sphere of production and the market do not hold.

As a result of these concessions on the theoretical front, the battle has now shifted to the arena of technical testing. As Charles Ferguson concludes in his survey of neoclassical theory (1969): "The question that confronts us is not whether the Cambridge Criticism is theoretically valid. It is. Rather, the question is an empirical or an econometric one: is there sufficient substitutability within the system to establish the neoclassical results?" As all who have reached this juncture well know, econometric hypothesis testing will neither quickly nor easily, if ever, yield unambiguous answers to this question.

An uncertain and ambiguous situation like this arises in a discipline such as economics for various reasons, the most important being the "softness" of data and questions of the interpretation of test results. Thus, for example, whenever hypotheses are not confirmed, it can usually be argued that the data required (additional) adjustment, or that other data should have been used, and/or that the *ceteris paribus* assumption was violated due to "exogenous" events which in turn require that additional or different assumptions be "ad hoc'ed" onto the test model, and so forth. Thus it happens that seeking refuge in the logical-positivistic argument that empirical outcomes are all that matter, not only begs the question, but is itself a metaphysical rather than a scientific position. As a salient example of this, Ferguson, after calling for econometric testing so as to determine the validity of the Cambridge criticisms of neoclassical production theory, went so far as to state that: "Until the econometricians have the answer for us, placing reliance upon neoclassical economic theory is a matter of faith. I personally have faith; but at present the best I can do to convince others is to invoke the weight of Samuelson's authority."

Metaphysics, as we have noted, plays an important and, in the Schumpeterian frame, a necessary role in the *pre*-analytic stage of theory formulation. However, its *constructive* utility at the later level of supposedly scientific explanation is an entirely different matter. Metaphysics was never intended to be a device for (theoretic) crisis management!

Some policy implications

Thus the reswitching anomaly, along with its theoretical developments and implications, has been placed in abeyance. And so it must be, for if this criticism were taken as being no less applicable to the real world than to the theoretical, then it follows, as already noted, that orthodox economics is unable to make any reliable statements concerning the relation of production to the various input markets. That is, the neoclassical vision of a market-coordinated production system, along with derivative growth and distribution theories, are all invalidated. As a consequence, the nature of the entire traditional circular flow conception is called into question.

The importance of the foregoing for policy is that the neoclassical vision of the circular flow provides much of the theoretic undergirding for the currently embattled version of

"Keynesianism" based on the so-called "neoclassical synthe-sis"—that is, the placing of major policy emphasis on the in-direct tools of fiscal and monetary policies so as to affect purposively, through microeconomic market responses, vari-ous key macroeconomic objectives, namely, production and employment, the price level, and balance in external pay-ments.

It is one thing to say that this conception of indirect eco-nomic management does not satisfactorily achieve its goals because of the existence of such real-world problems as bottlenecks, power, premature inflation, inflationary ex-pectations, random shocks, ratchet and spillover effects, and the like. In such situations, an economically coherent and consistent market-based system of production and distribu-tion is still assumed to exist, though it is overlaid with po-litical, institutional, and psychological factors that affect eco-nomic adjustments and performance. The basic strategy, in this case, would be to maintain the general neoclassical-syn-thetic emphasis on fiscal and monetary management (with perhaps somewhat greater stress on the monetary tool, if the monetarists were to have their way), and supplement these tools with finely targeted direct and specific devices—for ex-ample, stricter antitrust enforcement, more sharply focused incentive (and disincentive) taxes, expanded job training and subsidization programs—so as to allow and encourage the ef-fective functioning of centerpiece fiscal and monetary devices.

It is quite another thing to argue that key markets in the system, particularly those in the resource or input sector, do not possess the fundamental economic characteristics neces-sary to the orderly systematic functioning that is postulated by mainstream theory. In this case, the entire production sys-tem, as envisioned by neoclassical economics, has lost its uni-fying consistency and coherence. Thus the neoclassical para-digm, summed up in the vision-laden analogy of an ordered circular flow among various markets, no longer reliably explains how production takes place and how the system as a whole functions. The implications of this for economic management are, of course, profound, though none of it means that policy approaches, or even textbooks for that matter, are soon to be changed. As we have noted, the *theoretical* Cambridge Criticism has been converted into a "positivistic" *empirical* question of whether or not there exists in the system enough substitutability to bring about neoclassical results.

But what if the Cambridge Criticism is valid, experientially as well as theoretically? Or to put the question in more usual terms: What if we do accept the extreme (logical-positivistic) methodological position—that a theory is tested not by its underlying (explanation of) structural relationships, but only by its empirical outcomes—and neoclassical production theory is empirically rejected or, what is more likely, found to be nonoperational in the result-oriented world of policy? What then?

In this eventuality, it then becomes the case that, although the modern market economy is indeed ordered in some way— otherwise its functioning would be random and more unstable than it actually is—the essence of critical relationships, particularly those on the production side, is not explained in any meaningful sense. An economy so "unexplained" is obviously not predictable and thus not amenable to the current "means→end" techniques of indirect guidance and control. This is to say that there would be no reason to expect that any particular policy actions (means) would lead to desired results (ends) with any calculable degree of certitude, perhaps even with respect to direction of change. In short, a lack of coherence and consistency (theoretical and/or "experienced") in various of the critical functional market relationships postulated by orthodox theory would give rise to a situation wherein the current means→end approach to policy making would turn out to be either irrelevant or even counterproductive vis-à-vis desired ends. We would then be faced with this situation: if there were to be any attempt at meaningful economic management at all, it would have to be supported by something other than the orthodox vision of the economy. For as far as the orthodox vision is concerned now, (1) logically rigorous and complete theoretical consistency is absent; (2) empirical (statistical) testing in accordance with the standards of logical-positivistic methodology will almost surely remain an open (a begged and metaphysical) question for an indefinite future; and (3) as even casual observation of current real-world experience indicates, our ability to make and carry out policy will remain seriously deficient. In the following section we will attempt to gain some further insight as to why this unhappy situation may have come about.

The vision of Walras

The neoclassical idea of an interdependent market economy is elegantly expressed through the device of Léon Walras' general equilibrium model (1926). Indeed, Mark Blaug, in his *Economic Theory in Retrospect* (1962), has urged that we should "...remember that nearly all [orthodox] economics nowadays *is* Walrasian economics." This includes not only the notion of interrelationships between and among resource and product markets (as specifically examined by Walras himself), but also the more modern idea of the interrelated public sector-private sector duality of the neoclassical synthesis, noted above.

Because of this general "Walrasian" nature of current orthodox economics, it is both interesting and useful to attempt to explicate the particular vision on which Walras himself based his scientific endeavors. Such an attempt is not intended to be a mere exercise in what could be called psycho-economics; if it were, it probably would, and should, have little impact on serious students of economics. Yet, it may

not be an overstatement to assert that practically every economist has some idea of what Walras is all about. And most
economists, if queried, would be inclined to accept the statement that what Walras essentially did was to articulate rigor-
ously the notion—the vision, as it were—of how an interrelated market economy could be expected to function automatically given the idealized situation of perfect competition
—that is, a competitive regime including perfect mobility of
resources, perfect flexibility in prices, and perfect information concerning prices as provided by a hypothetical "auc-
tioneer." This interpretation of Walras' vision and consequent
scientific achievement would be quite consistent with the
present-day notion of Walrasian economics as exemplified in
the neoclassical synthesis. That is, given competitive assumptions, particular economic means will exert consistent and
predictable forces toward certain economic ends. This means
that direct or indirect policy actions, affecting the economy's
price signposts, either absolutely or relative to one another,
could be expected to exert forces that would tend to move
the economy toward particular and expectable economic
adjustments. If this were not the case, the problem would be
that the economy in some way failed to meet the assumptions
of the model—for example, that there were "frictions"; imperfect information, particularly affecting expectations about
an uncertain future; all other things were not equal in that
random shocks or exogenous forces shifted against given economic variables; and so forth. . . .

The key point in the above argument turns on the inherent
consistency and predictability of market-oriented economic
forces, meaning that particular economic means could be
taken as precedent to particular economic ends, *ceteris
paribus*. The question at this juncture is: Does this vision, the
essence of this idea-system, square with Walras' own, and
with what he thought he was doing in articulating his formal
(scientific) model?

According to an astute student of Walras, William Jaffé, the answer to that question appears to be no. As Jaffé recently pointed out (1977), Walras' purpose in searching for a general equilibrium solution to market system interrelationships was to see if such a condition was logically possible, that is, to try to discern whether such a condition was internally consistent and whether its existence was possible. Walras' purpose, according to Jaffé, was *not* to describe or to analyze a real-world system, even under stringent assumptions. His goal then was not positivistic; rather it was essentially normative. Walras was attempting to find out whether an economic system based upon conditions that to his mind constituted economic justice, both in exchange and distribution, *could* exist at any given time. He was thus primarily concerned with a particular end, a vision of a "just" terminal state; he was not exploring the functional relationships that would lead to this state in the means→end sense of modern orthodox economics. As Jaffé puts it: "Walras's aim even in his 'pure economics' was prescriptive or normative rather than positive or descriptive. His object was to formulate [invent?] an economic system in conformity with an ideal of social justice."

Thus if nearly all of modern economics is Walrasian, as Blaug states, then it appears that nearly all of modern economics has little to do with the nature and purpose of Walras' own vision and scientific endeavors.

Policy-theory inversion: a possible framework

Walras thus appears as primarily concerned with the existential nature of a particular end state. More recently, Adolph Lowe (1977), continuing in this vein, has centered his work within the conception of the interrelated market-type system. However, because of the problematic nature of market feedback effects, he has explicitly rejected the neoclassical concept of means→end economics in favor of what he calls "Political Economics," or the instrumental "end→means" approach to economic policy and analysis.

In Lowe's conception it becomes the task of politics to determine a set of ends or goals which comprise a desired terminal or end state for the economy. It then becomes the task of economics to determine if the end state is internally consistent, that is, possible, and if so then, taking this state as datum, to regress, directing investigation toward the discovery of the interrelationships among the particular determinants that comprise the paths to the stipulated goals. As Lowe has recently put it (1976): ". . .what is perhaps the most startling feature of Political Economics [is] its assertion *that only 'prior ordering' of reality itself can provide us with a tractable object of theoretical investigation*" (emphasis added).

This end→means instrumental approach to ordering economic reality quite obviously connotes national economic planning. But even more, it is a particular approach to planning that is geared to and based on particular aspects of market-oriented economic theory and of its envisioned corollary economic system. Primary among these aspects is the unknown, and perhaps unknowable or even nonexistent, ordering of economic variables and relationships. Thus, the orthodox neoclassical-synthetic approach, even when it includes direct intervention in the system here and there so as to improve or otherwise affect market function, cannot be useful as the basic prescriptive approach to the achievement of various pronounced policy goals.

Also, the end→means instrumental argument makes much of the current debate about national economic planning either irrelevant or superfluous. For if the modern market economy, or the theory that purports to explain it, contains inherent features that interfere with consistent "rational" adjustment, then the pertinent question for economic policy cannot be "if" there should be national planning, but rather "when," "how" and "for whom."

It is ironical that a planning philosophy, such as outlined above, could give theoretical and operational reality to aspects of orthodox theory and practice that are now under strong suspicion. For example, to the extent that traditional optimization and maximization criteria, such as "efficiency" and "welfare," are incorporated as features of the envisoned end state, orthodox analysis and technique will gain much in meaning and relevance. And the neoclassical apparatus could play the unexpected role of achieving the planning goals of a type of "socialism" rather than, as now, prescribing the (indirect) managerial techniques for our type of (mixed) "capitalism." And such a turn, it appears, would be consistent with Walras' own view of economics—indeed, even more so than is the so-called "Walrasian" economics of current orthodoxy.

ALESSANDRO RONCAGLIA

The Sraffian Contribution

Sraffa's 1960 book, *Production of Commodities by Means of Commodities*, has been cited as playing a decisive role in the development of post-Keynesian theory. Since the precise nature of Sraffa's contribution to the reconstruction of economic theory along non-neoclassical lines is not always clearly specified, and the scope and conceptual framework of his analysis have remained somewhat obscure, this essay will attempt to place Sraffa's work in proper perspective in relation to post-Keynesian theory. It will cover, among other topics, the development of Sraffa's analysis; the distinction between his classical representation of the economic process, based on the notion of a "surplus," and the neoclassical vision, and some specific results of his analysis—in particular, the distinction between basic and nonbasic commodities, and the standard system.

These various features of Sraffa's analysis fall within the classical tradition, but this does not mean that they are indissolubly connected to nineteenth-century economic conditions. In fact, as will be pointed out below, post-Keynesian pricing theory, with the importance it attaches to the mark-up above costs, can be accommodated within the framework of Sraffa's analysis. While there are many other issues still to be resolved before the Sraffian and post-Keynesian approaches can be fully integrated, it is along these lines that a new mode of economic analysis, with far-reaching political implications, is being worked out by a number of economists all over the world.

Development of Sraffa's analysis

Sraffa's critical analysis of neoclassical value theory started in the 'twenties. In an article published in Italian in 1925, discussing the Marshallian theory of the firm, Sraffa criticized one of the key underpinnings of neoclassical theory. This is the idea that costs are directly related to the quantity produced, so that when the quantity produced increases, costs per unit of output first decrease (the principle of increasing returns) and then increase (the principle of decreasing returns). But these two principles, as Sraffa noted, were originally introduced into classical political economy for two quite different purposes. On the one hand, the principle of increasing returns was based on the enhanced productivity that was thought to derive from the effect which any greater division of labor has in expanding markets, and therefore was related to the theory of accumulation presented in Adam Smith's *The Wealth of Nations*. On the other hand, the principle of decreasing returns was associated with the differential rent that was thought to arise from the extension of cultivation to less and less fertile lands, and therefore was related to the theory of distribution developed in David Ricardo's *Principles*. The point of Sraffa's criticism was not just that Marshall, in basing his microeconomic analysis of value and distribution on these principles, was mixing two disparate concepts, each derived from a different source. Even more important —the concepts themselves violate the *ceteris paribus* assumptions of Marshall's partial equilibrium analysis, and thus, when combined, they involve a logical inconsistency.

Between 1925 and 1960, when *Production of Commod-*

ities by Means of Commodities finally appeared, Sraffa expanded the scope of his criticism of neoclassical value theory while working to perfect his analysis of prices and distribution along classical lines. Leaving aside the neoclassical framework and turning to the classical tradition, Sraffa had to tackle a problem which Ricardo had been unable to solve in a rigorous way, one which Ricardo had tried to circumvent with his labor theory of value. (This involved the argument that the prices of different commodities are proportional to the quantities of labor required to produce them.) Ricardo's problem was that prices depend on how the national surplus product is distributed among social classes, that is, mainly between wages and profits, while the surplus itself cannot be measured without first knowing the prices of the commodities that make it up. In *Production of Commodities by Means of Commodities*, Sraffa solves this problem of circularity by showing that "the distribution of the surplus must be determined through the same process and at the same time as are the prices of production." Analytically, the solution is given by a set of equations, one for every sector or commodity produced by the system. Each equation requires that the product of the sector (the quantity produced multiplied by the price of the commodity) is equal to costs plus profits on the value of capital advanced. In each equation, costs are given by the required quantities of the various means of production, labor included, each multiplied by its price; profits are computed at the ruling uniform rate prevailing in the system. The entire set of equations can be regarded as showing the prices which must prevail if the system is not only to yield a surplus but also to reproduce itself over time. The distribution of the surplus can be determined in one of two ways: (1) by assuming, as the classical writers like Ricardo did, that the workers receive only a subsistence wage—in which case all the surplus accrues, in the form of profits, to the capitalist class which owns the capital goods;

or (2) by assuming that part of the surplus is distributed to workers in the form of wages which exceed the subsistence level. In the latter case, any increase in the amount of the surplus going to the workers in the form of a higher real wage will be at the expense of the capitalists' profits. Changes in distribution of the surplus between wages and profits imply changes in relative prices because of "the inequality of the proportions in which labor and means of production are employed in the various industries." Thus prices are determined by the technological conditions of production and by the manner in which the surplus is distributed between wages and profits.

The concept of surplus

Sraffa's analysis, as outlined above, is based on a concept which was central to classical political economy, from its origins in the seventeenth-century works of William Petty to the nineteenth-century writings of Ricardo and Mars. This is the concept of surplus—that is, the excess of commodities produced over the quantities of the same commodities required for their production. The recognition of these intellectual antecedents allows us to outline the conceptual framework within which Sraffa's analysis of prices and distribution emerged.

Productive economic activity was conceived by the classical economists as a circular or repetitive process. Each cycle, that is, each period of production (say, a year) begins with given amounts of the various requisite commodities at the disposal of the producing units (the firms). These commodities are then utilized, during the production process, either as means of production or as means of subsistence for the workers. At the end of the period, in the system as a whole, there is an excess or surplus, which (assuming subsistence wages) is distributed to the two dominating classes of society, either to the capitalists as profits or to the landlords as rents. But, at the end of the period, each productive unit has in its possession only the particular commodity which it produces. Before starting a new production cycle, the other commodities required for production must be acquired through the market by giving in exchange part of its own production for the output of other producing units. The surplus of whichever commodity is produced is also sold in the market, in order that profits and rents can be distributed to the individual capitalists and landlords in money terms. At the same time, these incomes are utilized in the market by the nonproductive classes to buy subsistence and luxury goods, and by the capitalists to buy the new means of production (which they are able to appropriate due to the fact that they have a share in the surplus product of society) to expand output in the succeeding periods. If wages are not paid in kind, workers similarly acquire their means of subsistence on the market from the various firms which thereby are able to recover the money they advanced to the workers as wages.

The market distribution of output therefore appears as a particular stage in an ever revolving cycle of production and reproduction. At one and the same time, the market insures the redistribution of commodities from the firms which produced them to the firms which will utilize them as means of production, and also insures the "realization" of profits and rents (and wages, if not paid in kind), allowing capitalists and landlords (and possibly workers) to choose their preferred commodity mix.

The set of exchange ratios (or relative prices) which are thereby established in the market must satisfy two conditions. They must be such as to insure the reintegration of the means of production of all firms (that is, they must cover production costs), and at the same time they must be compatible with the principles regulating the distribution of the surplus product within the two classes of landlords and capitalists. In the Sraffian analysis, as in the Ricardian theory, these principles give rise to differential rent among landowners on the basis of the different fertility of lands and to a uniformity in the rate of profit on the capital advanced in all sectors (an analytical hypothesis which corresponds to the assumption of free competition).

The neoclassical approach

This conceptual background, which is common to classical economists and to Sraffa, was replaced by a completely different one with the advent of neoclassical (or marginalist) theory, which has been for the past century, and still is, the dominant academic paradigm. The basic classical vision of production as a circular process was replaced in neoclassical theory by the conception of a one-way process, starting from the availability of scarce resources and ending with satisfaction of consumers' tastes. Economics, according to neoclassical theorists, was to become an exact science like physics, concerned with the optimal allocation of scarce resources among alternative ends. Within such a framework, the objective approach to value (based on the physical costs of production) which prevailed in classical political economy was supplanted by a subjective approach, based on consumers' tastes (utility maps). The concept of a surplus over the inputs necessary for production disappeared; the theory of distribution was no longer concerned with the division of such a surplus among the leading classes of society, but rather became a particular application of price theory, related to the "prices" of the various "factors of production" (land, labor, and capital in the first instance, but all the various physically different means of production in the more rigorous "general" version of the theory). Relative prices came to be interpreted as "indicators of relative scarcities" of the various goods, instead of being viewed as the ratios to which a regular repetition of the production process was linked.

All the major exponents of marginal theory, from Walras to Böhm-Bawerk and Wicksell, in an attempt to say something useful about the real world, tried to explain the determination of the profit rate (which, in their models, was the same as the interest rate) within the general framework of their theories. The profit, or interest, rate was thus presented as the price of a particular commodity, "capital." Applying the general framework of supply and demand, it was asserted that an increase in the price of capital (that is, the profit or interest rate) would bring about an increase in supply of, and a decrease in demand for, the commodity "capital." But such reasoning, to avoid circularity, requires a measure of "capital" which does not depend on how income is distributed between wages and profits. Sraffa, in *Production of Commodities by Means of Commodities*, shows that such a measure cannot exist. A similar argument is to be found in the work of Garegnani (1960).

This criticism of the concept of capital used in marginal analysis extends to the version of neoclassical theory so common in applied economics, the one in which an aggregate production function is derived, linking variations in output to variations in the "quantities" of capital and labor utilized, and with the profit and wage rates determined on marginalist principles. Since Joan Robinson's 1953 article, "The Production Function and the Theory of Capital," debates in capital theory have centered on this aggregate version. Yet Sraffa's critique (and Garegnani's in 1960) is more general and basic, for it refers to any attempt, within both partial and general equilibrium analysis, to determine the equilibrium profit rate within the context of long-period marginalist (neoclassical) theory.

The classical problems

As already indicated, Sraffa's book not only provides the basis for a critique of neoclassical theory; it also contains an analysis of prices along classical lines. There are two classical problems in particular to which Sraffa gives a definitive solution: (1) the distinction between necessary and luxury commodities; and (2) the definition of an "invariable" standard of value. Let us examine each of these points.

The distinction between "necessaries" and "luxuries" (according to the terminology in use at the time) was introduced by the English classical economists in order to differentiate between those commodities whose conditions of production influenced the entire system of relative prices and the relationship between the wage rate and the rate of profits, and those which had no such overall significance. In the framework commonly adopted by the classical economists, the wage is fixed in physical terms and as given quantities of particular commodities. These "wage goods," together with the goods directly or indirectly utilized as their means of production, are then the "necessary commodities."

Sraffa, avoiding the assumption of a wage rate given in physical terms, introduces a slightly different distinction, signaled by his different terminology. He distinguishes between basic and nonbasic products, that is, between those commodities that enter directly or indirectly as means of production in *all* processes of production, and those commodities which do not serve as means of production or which are used, directly or indirectly, in only a limited number of processes. This distinction is entirely based on technology: for those wage goods which are not also "technologically" basic products, there will be no general repercussion on the system due to a change in their conditions of production. This will be the case if the change in their prices does not produce a change in the prevailing wage rate.

The distinction between basic and nonbasic products, though strictly valid only in the formal analysis of the prices of production, is probably a tool whose (cautious) application might prove useful in a number of policy problems, such as the regulation of prices, anti-inflation programs, and the incidence on prices of various kinds of taxes. For example, escalator clauses, which link money wage rates to the money prices of a basket of wage goods, could be interpreted as treating those goods as "basic," bringing the analysis back to the classical distinction between necessary and luxury goods.

The standard commodity

Entirely theoretical, on the other hand, is the device of the "standard commodity," by which Sraffa delimited and solved a problem which had perplexed Ricardo up to the end of his life. Ricardo tried to use a single standard of value, that of labor embodied in commodities, to deal with two different and distinct problems. The first problem relates to the identification of the change in the "value" of specific commodities due to a change in the methods of production, which lead, in turn, to changes in relative prices. The second is to distinguish such changes in relative prices from those which are caused by a change in the distribution of income. The first problem requires the definition of an "absolute" standard of value, such as labor contained; the second is solved by Sraffa's device of the standard commodity.

The standard commodity is a theoretical construct, rather than an actual good. It is a composite commodity, with the different goods which comprise it weighted in the same proportion as the goods required to produce it. The standard commodity therefore has the same technical coefficients as the whole of its means of production; and, as a result, a change in wages will, in the case of the standard commodity, be offset by an equal and opposite change in profits. The same will not be true for other commodities. Thus, a change in the price of the other commodities, relative to the price of the standard commodity, will be due entirely to the effect that a change in income distribution has on their costs of production. In this way, the standard commodity serves as a baseline against which to measure the effect that a change in the distribution of income between wages and profits has on relative prices.

Competition and oligopoly

Thus there is a conceptual background common both to classical political economy and to Sraffa's analysis of prices of production and related problems. Prices of production, being by definition those relative prices which give rise to a uniform rate of profit throughout all sectors of the economy, are based on the classical assumption of free competition, insured by the freedom of new firms to enter any sector. What, then, is the meaning of this assumption, under modern conditions of mass production and mark-up pricing?

Under the oligopolistic conditions which prevail in the industrial sector (that is, in manufacturing), money prices are fixed by dominant firms, acting as price leaders in their respective industries. In determining prices, and especially in continuously adapting them to variations in costs, these price leaders add to unit direct costs a margin (mark-up) designed to cover fixed costs and to allow a certain unit rate of profit. The higher the barriers to entry in the sector under consideration, the higher the rate of profit which generally emerges as a result of following the mark-up formula. It might therefore seem that the dominant firms, acting on the basis of the finance required to implement their investment plans, are able to use their market power to determine their profits at will. However, this would be a misleading representation of the process of competition under oligopoly.

The fact is that the pricing discretion of dominant firms in oligopolistic industries is limited by fear of new competitors entering their markets, attracted by the unusually high profit margins. While it is true that these margins are likely to be higher than they are in competitive industries, still, as the work of Joe Bain (1956, 1958) and Paolo Sylos-Labini (1962) on oligopolistic markets shows, this is simply due to the barriers hindering the entry of new firms. These barriers may reflect technological factors, such as the minimum size of plants necessary to achieve the lowest possible costs; or they may be due to social and institutional factors, such as the brand loyalty among consumers which imposes on newcomers the cost of acquiring a share in the market. These factors, however, merely limit, they do not preclude, entry into the sector. The dominant firms are therefore restricted in their quest for maximum profits by potential competition, and they are able to obtain a rate of profit higher than the one prevailing in competitive markets only within a well delimited range, depending on the significance of existing barriers to entry. Thus the general (competitive) rate of profit remains a useful point of reference even for oligopolistic firms. The deviation of any firm's or sector's rate from the average profit rate simply reflects technological or institutional factors. These factors can be taken as given in the analysis of relative prices, and are simply a second approximation to reality, logically following the investigation of prices of production.

With this fact in mind, Sraffa's analysis, though conducted along classical lines under the competitive assumption of a uniform rate of profits, is not incompatible with modern oligopolistic conditions; and indeed can readily be integrated with non-neoclassical theories of oligopolistic behavior. Moreover, Sraffa's rejection of marginal theory is a necessary preliminary step before a complete and adequate explanation for the level of aggregate economic activity can be offered. In fact, after considering the implications of Sraffa's analysis, it would appear that the problem of aggregate demand is best handled as two separate problems: one, the problem of determining levels of output (which are taken as given in

Sraffa's analysis so that their determination is logically prior to the problem of prices); and the other, the problem of "realization," or how the sale of the quantities produced can be assured. This opens the way for the introduction of the Keynesian concept of effective demand which coincides with, and offers a possible solution to, the first of the two problems just mentioned. It would thus appear that Sraffa's analysis offers a basis for a theoretical integration of the classical, Marxian, and post-Keynesian traditions.

Policy implications

This brings us to the policy, and political, implications of Sraffa's analysis. The main impact is at the ideological level. As already pointed out, competitive prices are seen by marginal theory as providing an optimal solution to an eternal problem, that of scarce means relative to ends. This mode of analysis also extends to the problem of distribution, with the variables, profit rate and wage rate, seen as the prices of the "factors of production"—capital and labor, respectively. A deviation (a rise, for example) in the real wage rate from the optimal level (due, say, to a deviation from perfect competition in the labor market caused by the existence of trade unions) is bound to provoke unemployment. Under such conditions (described by a certain technology, a certain set of consumers' tastes, and a certain stock of resources), there is a "natural" and *optimal* level of the distributive variables, and the trade union's struggle over the distribution of income loses all meaning. Indeed, class struggle in general loses its meaning as well. The implication is that the distribution of income cannot be altered, through political activity, without the material conditions of life being adversely affected.

   This ideological implication of the marginal analysis, together with the theory of value and distribution on which it relies, must be viewed with skepticism in the face of Sraffa's criticisms. The way is thus open for an alternative analysis of distribution, centered on the opposition of wages and profits. This has widespread consequences for economic policy. As an example, the Sraffian wage-profit relationship and the distinction between basic and nonbasic commodities can be used to clarify a specific problem relating to incomes policy, this being the importance of the basket of wage-goods chosen as the basis for escalator clauses.

At the same time, Sraffa's solution to the classical and Marxian problems of how prices of production are determined, and their relationship with the distribution of income between wages and profits, clears up one of the main difficulties in the classical tradition. This points to the possibility of developing a new political economy along the lines, and within the limits, indicated by the classical economists and Marx; that is, by taking into account the historically relative nature of the capitalistic mode of production and the class struggle inherent in it.

EILEEN APPELBAUM

The Labor Market

The labor aspects of post-Keynesian theory have yet to be systematically developed. Still, as this essay will attempt to show, it is possible to combine some widely agreed upon tenets of post-Keynesian thought, such as the importance of the oligopoly sector, the nature of technology in industrialized countries, and the process of price formation by firms, with the work that has been done by American institutional economists, particularly with regard to segmented labor markets. The result of this synthesis is a fairly comprehensive analysis of the labor market that largely follows Keynes in its approach to the demand for labor, and the segmented labor market theorists in its approach to the supply of labor. A post-Keynesian analysis of this sort leads to a conclusion radically different from the orthodox, neoclassical theory. This is that neither the demand for labor nor the supply of labor depends on the real wage. It follows from this that the labor market is not a true market, for the price associated with it, the wage rate, is incapable of performing any market-clearing function, and thus variations in the wage rate cannot eliminate unemployment.

The orthodox theory of wage determination and unemployment

The conventional analysis of the demand for labor by the firm proceeds on the basis of three fundamental assumptions. The first is that firms always act to maximize profits, even in the short run. The second is that firms are able to combine labor and capital in any proportion whatever, and that firms can alter the capital-labor mix every time the relative price of capital and labor changes. Finally, it is assumed that firms are price-takers in the market for labor and other factors of production, and that therefore they view wage rates as given. Under these circumstances it follows that the demand for labor by the firm is given by the familiar rule, "hire labor up to the point at which the value of the output produced by the last worker employed just equals the money wage which he or she must be paid." The firm's demand for labor thus depends on the contribution to production of the last worker hired (reflecting the marginal product of labor); on the price which the firm receives for its output; and on the money wage which it must pay. Ignoring the aggregation problems involved in generalizing from the individual firm to the entire economy, orthodox theory utilizes the same method of analysis to derive the economy-wide demand for labor, which is viewed as varying inversely with the ratio of the money wage rate to the price level—that is, with real wages.

The conventional analysis of labor supply is based on the following assumptions: that work represents a sacrifice for which the worker must be compensated; that the individual's (or, in some formulations, the household's) well-being is related to the hours of leisure and to the purchasing power of income; and that each worker (or household) is attempting to maximize his, her (or its) well-being. Given their initial endowments of wealth, the money wage rates they can command, and the price level, it is argued that workers will find that some combinations of leisure time and purchasing power will be attainable while others will not. Each worker will then choose to supply that number of hours of labor which maximizes his or her well-being. The individual's labor supply decision thus depends on money wages and the price level. If workers immediately calculate the full effect of price level changes on purchasing power, then the hours of labor supplied by the individual will be an increasing function of the ratio of the money wage rate to the price level (that is, of real wages). The aggregate quantity of labor supplied can then be obtained by adding up the individual supply curves, and it is positively related to the real wage rate.

Having thus derived both aggregate labor demand and labor supply as functions of the real wage rate, the standard macroeconomic analysis of employment proceeds to demonstrate that, in the absence of rigid money wages, supply and demand in the labor market would simultaneously determine real wages and the level of employment. It is convenient in arguing the point to begin with the commodity, money, and labor markets in balance and then consider the effects of a decline in autonomous spending. Immediately following the decline in spending, the amount of output sold·in markets will be less than the full-employment level of output that firms have been producing. Initially, however, firms do not know this and continue to produce the full-employment level of output. With the supply of output greater than the demand, prices will, so the traditional argument goes, fall. With money wages unchanged, the real wage will rise. As a result, the demand for labor will fall while the supply of labor increases. If money wages were flexible downward, this excess of supply over demand would cause money wages to fall. The decline in prices and money wages would, in turn, reduce the demand for money. Needing less money for day-to-day transactions, households and firms would try to buy bonds, thus bidding up bond prices and forcing down interest rates. Lower interest rates would encourage an increase in investment spending, and output and employment would both rise. Ultimately, equilibrium would be restored in the vicinity of the full-employment level of output, with prices, money wages, and interest rates lower, and real wages virtually unaffected. The problem, as it is usually presented, is that money wages are not flexible downward, and thus involuntary unemployment must ensue.

The conclusion that some level of involuntary unemployment will have to be tolerated follows immediately from the "neoclassical synthesis" of Keynesian and pre-Keynesian arguments. If the money wage rate were flexible, this analysis suggests, real wage rates could adjust and would serve to equate the supply of and demand for labor. That is, flexible wages would act as a market-clearing mechanism capable of eliminating excess supply or demand in the labor market. Market forces alone would tend to reestablish full employment; government policies to reduce involuntary unemployment would be unnecessary. However, with money wages rigid, even orthodox economists embrace the Keynesian view that government intervention in the economy is needed to offset any decline in autonomous spending and restore full employment. Fiscal policies to increase aggregate demand directly and monetary policies to reduce the rate of interest and thereby increase investment will, even according to orthodox analysis, reduce unemployment. Unfortunately, according to the orthodox economists, Keynesian economics is "depression economics"—Keynesian solutions can be safely utilized only during major recessions or depressions. At other times, policies that increase aggregate demand and reduce unemployment will raise the demand for labor, thereby driving up the money wage rate (which, according to the orthodox view, is determined in the labor market by supply and demand) and generating inflation. The result is a Phillips curve trade-off between unemployment and inflation. Thus orthodox economics suggests that some unemployment must be tolerated in order to keep inflation within reasonable bounds.

The post-Keynesian critique

As Sidney Weintraub has observed (1978), "Keynes' entire intellectual commitment was to use reason to eradicate economic ailments rather than to 'trade-off' one ill for another." Based on this heritage, post-Keynesian economists reject the view that the goals of stable prices and full employment are irreconcilable. As we have seen, orthodox economists view rigid money wages as the major cause of unemployment. They argue that if money wages would decline whenever aggregate demand fell, real wages would also be reduced, and the volume of employment would increase. Furthermore, orthodox economists contend that real wages must be increased in order to entice more people to work. Since they believe that bargaining over money wages determines real wages, they argue that firms that wish to hire more workers will have to pay higher money wages. Any increase in the demand for labor will, in their view, result in rising money wages. It is this argument that leads orthodox economists to the conclusion that price stability and low unemployment cannot be achieved simultaneously. Post-Keynesian economists, however, reject this theory of wage determination.

The arguments of modern-day orthodoxy were answered long ago by Keynes (1936). Keynes objected to the twin ideas, (1) that real wages depend on the money wage bargain reached between workers and firms, and (2) that labor can reduce its real wage and increase the volume of employment by accepting a lower money wage. Even if the general tenor of orthodox theory were accepted, Keynes pointed out, these two propositions would not follow. A reduction in the general level of money wages, after all, will reduce marginal cost. At the going market prices for outputs, therefore, each firm will want to produce more. As the supply of products of all kinds increases, the orthodox view teaches that the general level of prices will fall. With both money wages and prices falling, the effects on the real wage are likely to be small. Even in the context of orthodox economic models, therefore, changes in money wages are not likely to be effective in altering real wages.

Keynes himself argued that in the short period money wages and real wages are subject to separate influences, and may even move in opposite directions. Post-Keynesians have argued that money wages depend largely on the respective bargaining power of business and labor, and on the normative factors reflected in what Alfred Eichner (1976) has termed the incremental wage pattern, or key wage bargain. Commodity prices, meanwhile, depend on the market power of firms and their need for internal funds to finance investment. Eichner and Jan Kregel (1975) have argued that if investment is increasing, so that there is a greater need for internal funds, while at the same time firms are optimistic about their ability to maintain a higher margin above costs, prices will rise relative to money wages and the real wage will be depressed. The real wage, thus, depends on the rate of investment and the pace of economic growth. A reduction in money wages would, in general, not be effective in increasing employment, since money wages and real wages need not move in the same direction. Depending on the extent to which prices also fell, real wages might rise, fall, or remain unchanged. Moreover, a decline in money wages relative to prices would tend to reduce consumption demand and hence employment; while a decline in both money wages and prices would tend to undermine business confidence and reduce investment demand and employment. Post-Keynesians conclude that rigid money wages are not the cause of involuntary unemployment.

Indeed, flexible money wages would subject firms to increased uncertainty and make planning more difficult without having much of an effect on either employment or real wages.

Keynes (1936), in replying to the argument that an increase in the demand for labor can only be met through an increase in money and real wage rates, noted that in general the volume of labor forthcoming at a given money wage depends on the availability of jobs. Furthermore, he observed, in the real world the supply of labor does not necessarily vary with changes in the real wage for, after all, labor is not in a position to withdraw its services with every increase in the price level, even though its real wage has been reduced. Keynes also noted that there have been wide variations in the level of employment without any apparent change in either the real wage or the productivity of labor. These real world outcomes are inconsistent with the argument that the demand for and supply of labor are functions of the real wage, and appear to contradict orthodox economic theory. Post-Keynesians, accordingly, have developed alternative theories of labor demand and labor supply.

Production and the demand for labor

The post-Keynesian argument relating the demand for labor to production has three components: the first conceptualizes the institutional nature of the business sector; the second characterizes the prevailing technology; while the third describes the pricing decisions of firms with market power. The demand for labor can then be related to the level of output that firms plan to produce without reference to marginal productivity theory.

The simplest assumption about the industrial structure of the United States that is reasonably close to reality is Robert Averitt's view (1968) that there exists a dual economy. That is, the American economy may be viewed as consisting of

(1) a set of core industries characterized by oligopolistic market structures; high capital-to-labor ratios; the use of sophisticated technology; substantial training costs for skilled, supervisory, and technical workers; high wages; the need for a literate and stable labor force; and the presence of strong trade union organizations, and (2) a periphery in which industries are characterized by their lack of market power; archaic management techniques; low capital requirements; low skill requirements; low wages, seasonal employment and/or an unstable work force; and little or no labor organization. Firms in the core are more likely to belong to industries in which concentration is extensive and, as a result, are more likely to have some control over output prices than are firms on the periphery. Prices set by firms in the core are sufficiently high to permit the replacement of used-up capital and the internal financing of a major part of any planned expansion, the payment of wages to workers that include a share of the social surplus, and the realization of a rate of profit that is higher than the average rate prevailing in the economy. Prices of commodities produced in the periphery tend to be depressed below their "normal" level. Firms can only keep prices down, however, by not replacing used-up capital, by paying workers lower wages, and/or accepting a lower rate of profit. Thus we observe in the nonoligopolistic industries numerous workers who, despite the fact that they work full time, must receive welfare payments in order to subsist. At the same time, the rate of profit on capital employed is typically below average and the existence of firms in this category often is most precarious.

Firms on the periphery do not compete for workers of a given quality on an equal basis with the oligopolistic firms in the core. In addition to higher wage rates, firms in the oligopolistic sector are able to offer workers better fringe benefits, greater job security, more opportunities for advancement and the protections which trade union organization affords. As a result, oligopolistic firms have a relatively permanent labor force attached to them. Workers laid off by such firms may seek interim employment elsewhere, but if production returns to its original level at the plant to which they are attached, they will return to the job they held there. For similar reasons, in periods of rapid growth, the oligopolistic sector is able to attract workers from the non-oligopolistic sector as it needs them.

Based on the assumption that factor inputs can be combined in any proportion, the conventional theory of the firm holds that output can be expanded only by combining increasing quantities of the variable inputs (labor and raw materials) with a fixed input (usually the capital stock but sometimes management skills). As production increases, the firm experiences first increasing and then decreasing output per unit of input, so that variable and marginal cost curves eventually increase with the rise in output. Rising marginal cost both limits the expansion of output by each firm (since no firm will produce an output for which marginal cost exceeds marginal revenue) and necessitates price increases as production expands. Price changes, according to this model, result largely from changes in demand.

Despite the widespread use of this model, it is applicable mainly to firms engaged in the production of raw materials and foodstuffs. In other enterprises, even in the short run, output can often be increased by adding a second shift of workers. Full utilization of capacity is more often the exception than the rule; and output is increased or decreased by varying the degree to which the inputs—both "fixed" and "variable"—are utilized, without any significant change in the proportions in which capital equipment and the "variable" inputs are combined. Indeed, a great deal of production takes place within firms characterized by fixed factor, or technical, coefficients that are not subject to change in the short run. Thus, over a broad range of output levels, average variable and marginal costs are constant, increasing only when full capacity utilization is approached.

In the short run, then, most firms can meet an increase in the demand for their product simply by increasing output at the prevailing cost level. The supply of output is elastic as a result of existing reserves of productive capacity, and "supply curves" are therefore horizontal. Prices cannot be determined in the usual manner, nor can firms maximize short-run profits by producing the level of output for which the marginal revenue to be earned is equal to the marginal cost. Decisions with respect to price and output must be arrived at in some other manner.

Modern versions of the mark-up pricing model used by Weintraub (1956, 1959), Eichner (1976), and others owe much to the work of the Polish economist Michal Kalecki (1954). In these models, average variable cost is constant, but average fixed cost decreases as production increases and overhead costs are spread over a greater volume of output. In setting price, therefore, firms must calculate average fixed and total cost per unit of output in advance, based on their estimates of the output that will be sold in the next period, or on some standard rate of plant utilization. Prices are usually established by adding to average variable cost a gross margin calculated to yield a target net profit should the firm actually sell the anticipated volume of output.

Variations in output, if they are moderate, leave price unchanged but do affect net profits. If the actual output sold is less than the estimated output, unit fixed costs will be higher than anticipated and net profits *ex post* will be less than the targeted amount. The reverse will occur if the output sold exceeds anticipated sales and the plant is operated more intensively than expected. While moderate changes in demand do not affect price, changes in money wage rates or in the prices of raw materials will generally cause prices to vary. Where a number of firms are engaged in producing for the same market, self-interest on the part of the firms commonly leads to the emergence of a price leader who effectively sets the market price of the product. This price will enable the leader to achieve its targeted profit when operating as anticipated, but other firms (which may be smaller or less efficient) may have higher costs and hence lower net profits.

Once prices have been established, the level of output which the firm produces in the short run is determined by the demand curve for the firm's output. Firms declare their price and they produce the output they believe the market will take. Firms motivated *not* by the goal of short-run profit maximization but by the wish to maintain or increase market share in a growing economy are likely to increase output rather than price when demand increases moderately and excess capacity is available. Of course, a large increase in anticipated sales for the products of a particular industry may generate a demand by firms for increased productive capacity. Firms in such industries may require more internally generated funds with which to finance investment, and may obtain such funds by increasing the margin above costs and setting a higher price. Thus a sustained increase in demand for an industry's output that is large enough to motivate firms to increase investment will eventually result in higher margins, if not higher prices. However, the usual marginal cost considerations do not enter here at all, and price does *not* vary with demand in a straightforward manner.

The various strands of the argument can be drawn together to explain the demand for labor. As part of the planning process, firms estimate expected GNP and project the corresponding level of anticipated industry-wide sales for the products they produce. Given the share of the market which it expects to command each firm then estimates the level of output which it expects to sell during the period for which plans are being made. Prices are set by means of a mark-up over average variable costs that will cover fixed costs at the planned output and will yield a targeted profit if that output is sold. Fixed technical coefficients in production imply that the demand for production workers by firms in both the periphery and the core of the economy is proportional to the level of output that the firm plans to produce, assuming there is excess capacity available so that the firm is on the horizontal segment of its cost curves. Managerial personnel and highly skilled technical and professional workers employed by firms in the core are usually viewed as quasi-fixed factors of production. Employment of these workers does not vary directly with the output the firm plans to produce. Instead, the firm requires some fixed number of overhead employees in order to operate each of its plants or plant segments. Utilizing a given plant or plant segment more or less intensively does not alter the number of such workers required by the firm. As production expands, however, so that additional plants are brought into operation, the demand for overhead workers will increase by discrete amounts. The aggregate demand for labor by the business sector can be obtained by summing up the demand by all individual firms, and it depends in a systematic manner on the expected aggregate demand for output.

Labor supply and underemployment

While much of the work that is performed in this society can be characterized as alienating or lacking in intrinsic rewards, the traditional analysis of the decision to supply labor ignores major dimensions of the labor supply process and yields conclusions that are at variance with observed reality. It is a somewhat distorted perspective which views the individual or household as weighing the disutility from additional work against the utility obtainable from the additional income thus earned, and offering fewer hours of labor or dropping out of the labor force entirely if real wages fall.

Eli Ginzberg (1976) has argued that work provides the individual with three essential kinds of satisfaction. First, whatever the level of real wages, employment of at least one family member is for most households the only available means of obtaining sufficient income to meet family needs. Necessity and the lack of practical alternatives compel households to continue to supply labor even in the face of a decline in real hourly earnings. Welfare payments, paid enrollment in manpower training programs and the possibility of obtaining income via quasi-legal hustles or criminal activities do provide alternative sources of remuneration but, as Bennett Harrison has argued (1977), these are meaningful alternatives to wage labor for only the most poorly paid workers. There is substantial mobility even then between the welfare rolls and low-wage employment. Secondly, employment provides the individual with purposeful activity and has a major impact on the individual's feelings of self-worth. Finally, though not all jobs give the individual a chance for development and training, employment nevertheless provides many individuals who are out of school with opportunities to utilize existing skills and develop new ones. Employment is important, therefore, for the income which the individual receives, for the contribution it makes to the individual's self-respect, and for its impact on the skill acquisition process. Very few households can afford to supply less labor as real wages decline; and an excess supply of labor cannot be eliminated in this manner.

The post-Keynesian analysis of unemployment draws heavily on the analyses of segmented labor markets advanced by radical economists like David Gordon (1972), Michael Reich and Richard Edwards (1973), the analysis of internal labor markets by Peter Doeringer and Michael Piore (1971), and the job competition model advanced by Lester Thurow (1975).

The labor market, in which workers compete for the

available jobs, is segmented into submarkets characterized by differences in wages, working conditions, and opportunities for advancement. To a large extent, labor market segmentation arose as part of the historical process which led to the development of technologically advanced, oligopolistic firms in industries at the core of the economy and smaller firms lacking technological sophistication on the periphery. The production processes of firms at the core have become increasingly complex, hierarchical, and interdependent. In this context many specific skills that workers need can only be learned through continuous tenure on a particular job or with a particular firm. Firms utilizing modern technologies thus have an incentive to encourage stable work histories for workers in jobs in which productivity is related to tenure both through adjustments in working conditions and monetary rewards and through a system of promotions to higher status jobs. Career ladders serve both to stratify workers and to keep them attached to the same firm for longer periods of time. It has thus become increasingly important for firms at the core to create differentiated job categories, whether they are required by technological change or not.

Encouraging stability on the part of the work force is costly to firms. Even firms at the core, therefore, have an incentive to restrict those extra expenses to as narrow a range of jobs as possible. Thus it is not surprising that even technologically advanced firms have created highly stratified internal job clusters with different entry requirements, with some strategic work sectors organized to encourage job stability and others to permit highly unstable work behavior. The labor market is, thus, segmented into a primary sector in which stable work habits are rewarded and a secondary sector in which turnover is high and stability is not required and often discouraged. Unemployment is concentrated among secondary sector workers and is related to the characteristics of their jobs rather than to wage rates.

Because testing new employees to determine potential job stability is difficult, employers have used superficial characteristics as an inexpensive screening device. They have tended, when filling the better jobs in which stability is important, to discriminate against those groups—blacks, women, teenagers —that historically have had unstable work patterns. Discrimination has set in motion a vicious cycle that guarantees that members of these groups will continue to experience high unemployment. Getting into the "right" job cluster has a critical effect on the training and advancement opportunities a worker receives. To the extent that skills must be obtained within the context of a specific job, discrimination against women, and against blacks and other minorities, restricts many of them to the lower strata of the labor market, denies them access to opportunities for job mobility and training, and confines them to the low end of both the skill and labor income distributions. The interaction between the characteristics of jobs in the secondary sector and the attitudes toward employment of workers with limited prospects has generated a high incidence of unemployment for women, as well as for blacks and other minorities.

Sex and ethnicity are not the only screening devices used to regulate entrance into the various segments of the labor market. Differences in class background and unequal access to educational institutions also function to limit entrance into jobs in the higher strata within the primary sector. Credentials requirements for those who are hired, together with subsequent promotions along an internal job ladder, serve both to shelter workers in the primary sector from the competition of other members of the labor force and to insulate the firm's wage structure from market forces. How rapidly workers are able to advance along their career ladders and how easily new graduates with the proper degrees and background will be absorbed into the primary sector depends on how rapidly the economy is expanding. Should the supply of highly trained and/or highly educated labor exceed the demand for such workers, it is not wage deflation but credentials inflation that will bring the supply of workers competing for jobs in the upper strata of the primary sector into line with existing job openings. Rising educational requirements for entrance into these jobs during periods of slow economic growth has the effect of thwarting the career aspirations of recent college and university graduates, who are bumped down into lower strata jobs in the primary sector and find few opportunities for advancement. Disappointment rather than unemployment is the price these workers pay.

The situation is quite different outside the primary sector of the labor market. With an excess supply of better educated young people, employment requirements for entry into the entire spectrum of jobs rise. Often, the level of certification has little to do with the actual requirements of the job; but certification is widely used by firms as an inexpensive screening device. The children of the poor, high school diplomas in hand, join the ranks of workers constrained by their own need for income and the limited number of primary sector jobs to seek poorly paying, unstable employment in the secondary sector of the labor market. Denied access to primary sector jobs, they can anticipate work experience marked by low earnings and a high incidence of unemployment. On the other hand, firms both on the periphery and at the core have available all the relatively unskilled manpower they need at the prevailing, low wage rate. No further reduction in wage rates is likely to reduce unemployment rates for workers in the secondary sector.

Summary

The labor market is not a "market" as that term is usually understood, for the labor market does not possess a market-clearing price mechanism. Variations in either money wages or in the real wage rate are unable to assure a zero surplus supply of labor, and thus eliminate unemployment. In the context of (1) an industrial structure that is largely oligopolistic, (2) fixed technical coefficients in production, and (3) mark-up pricing, the demand for labor depends on the level of aggregate economic activity. It has little, if anything, to do with the marginal product of labor. The supply of labor, meanwhile, depends largely on demographic and other sociocultural factors, though it is somewhat responsive to changes in employment opportunities. When aggregate demand falls below the potential output of the economy and unemployment increases, the personal qualifications required for entry into or advancement to a job in a given stratum of the labor market increase; and the educational gains of women, blacks, and others are devalued in the ensuing credentials inflation. The result is a queue of those awaiting access to the better jobs, or even to any job at all, that cannot be eliminated by a decline in real wages.

Conversely, while the demand for labor relative to the supply of labor plays a major role in establishing the level of money wages by strengthening or weakening labor's bargaining position, the growth of output and the solidarity of the trade union movement have an even larger impact. Of greater importance than the level of money wages, however, is the level of real wages. This, moreover, depends not only on money wages but on prices as well. When money wages increase faster than productivity, prices need to rise in order for the firm's margin above average variable costs to cover fixed costs and continue yielding targeted net profits. In periods of economic growth, if the margin above average variable costs rises as firms try to generate increased internal funds with which to finance investment, prices will rise relative to money wages. The growth of real wages may therefore be depressed below the growth in the average productivity of labor despite substantial gains in money wages. Thus, while conditions of slackness or tightness in the labor market play a role, neither money nor real wages can be said to be uniquely determined by the demand for and supply of labor.

Policy implications

The burden of the post-Keynesian argument is that wage determination and unemployment are two distinct processes and must be understood as such, and that wage rates do not serve, in most contexts, to equate the supply of labor with the demand for it. Thus, the labor market has no market-clearing mechanism—from which it follows that adjustments in wage rates cannot eliminate unemployment. The volume of employment depends on aggregate demand factors, not on wage rates. Techniques for regulating aggregate demand through government monetary and fiscal policies have been known at least since the publication of Keynes' *General Theory* in 1936. Reluctance to reduce unemployment through the use of such expansionary policies stems from the misguided view that a Phillips curve trade-off between inflation and unemployment exists. Increasing aggregate demand, it is feared, will lead not only to increases in the volume of employment but to higher money wages and prices as well. The fear of inflation has led public officials to pursue policies whose effect is to curtail the level of economic activity. It would seem that there has been sufficient experience with such policies in the last decade to convince even a skeptical observer that money wages and prices are largely unaffected by reductions in aggregate demand. Restrictive monetary and fiscal policies may keep unemployment high but they are ineffective in combating inflation. The resulting stagflation (high unemployment, high inflation) is an all too familiar outcome.

From the post-Keynesian perspective the primary cause of inflation is not excess demand for goods or labor, but rather the conflict over how the available income and output are to be distributed. Restrictive monetary and fiscal policies, by reducing the volume of income and output, merely heighten the struggle among megacorps, smaller firms, workers, and government over the distribution of income and output. There is clearly a need for public policies to assure that the economy continues to grow and that the national income is distributed in an acceptable manner. Implicit in this is the need for social and economic planning to determine the secular growth rate, to eliminate poverty, to improve the standard of living of workers and others, and to enable investment to take place at the appropriate socially determined rate. The difficult political questions raised by this approach should not be minimized. Safeguards would be required to insure that the development of goals and the implementation of plans would be subject to democratic control and responsive to social needs. Furthermore, such planning would result in socially imposed limits on the megacorp's ability to determine its own margin above costs and to make investment decisions. But such policies are necessary if economic growth, full employment, and a rising standard of living are not to be sacrificed in the attempt to end inflation by conventional means.

Finally, it must be recognized that whatever the rate of unemployment may be, the burden is not shared equally by all demographic groups. Layoffs and firings are associated primarily with the dead-end, low-wage jobs characteristic of the secondary labor market. As a result, blacks, women, and others who are overrepresented in the secondary labor market experience a disproportionate amount of unemployment as well. Ginzberg (1977) has calculated that between 1950 and 1976 the number of "poor" jobs increased much more rapidly than the number of "good" jobs: fewer than three out of every ten new jobs created by the private sector during that period were "good" jobs. Public policy to eliminate the poorest jobs and to create enough good jobs to allow for the upward mobility of women and blacks without displacing workers already in better jobs is clearly required. Again, difficult political and social questions are involved, for any substantial reduction in low-wage employment will require fundamental adjustments in consumption and production patterns throughout society.

BASIL J. MOORE

Monetary Factors

There is as yet no formal post-Keynesian theory of money that would correspond to the orthodox Keynesian or monetarist views on the subject. The consensus, such as it exists, is primarily negative rather than positive. However, by noting those key features of the prevailing orthodoxy which are explicitly rejected by the as yet relatively small group of post-Keynesian economists, it is possible to outline the distinguishing features of an alternative approach to monetary theory. These features include the serious recognition of historical time, with its implications for the rejection of general equilibrium analysis; the centrality of finance for investment behavior; the unique role of labor markets in the price determination process; and the endogeneity of the money stock resulting from the need of central banks to validate the rate of growth of money wages. The last means that the money stock both derives from economic processes and affects those processes.

Historical time

Perhaps the most basic point underlying the post-Keynesian position on money is that historical time must be taken seriously. A sharp distinction needs to be made between historical and logical time. For while logical time can move either forward or backward, historical time can only go forward. The essence of an economy that operates in historical time is that its past is given and cannot be changed, and that its future is uncertain and cannot be known. As Marshall warned in the preface of the first edition of his *Principles* (1890), "the element of Time is the centre of the chief difficulty of almost every economic problem."

In *The General Theory* (1936), one of Keynes' major efforts was to work out the implications of the uncertainty generated in historical time for much of what happens in an actual economy. A monetary economy, he argued, is not just a more complicated barter system. Rather, an economy with modern capitalist financial institutions behaves in a manner fundamentally different from what he called a "real exchange" —that is, a barter—economy. While Keynes' *A Treatise on Money* (1930) still belonged to the neoclassical tradition, focusing as it did on the manner of transition from one equilibrium position to another, *The General Theory* represented a paradigmatic shift. In the latter work, Keynes attempted to develop an analysis based on the fact that our lives are in fact spent in transition, and that in every transitory state, objective and subjective changes occur which in turn feed back to alter our future behavior. With hindsight, we may now view Keynes as wrestling with the difficult and analytically intractable problem of attempting to explain the dynamics of the disequilibrium process in which we are continually enmeshed.

Accordingly, one of the key theoretical constructs that post-Keynesians have reluctantly abandoned as useless for analyzing reality is "general equilibrium." The very concept of a position of balance towards which a system is tending, and from which there is no further tendency to change, is inappropriate to historical time. As Joan Robinson has insisted (1962), the metaphors usually given to illustrate the concept are all drawn from the dimension of space, where backwards and forwards motion is possible. But real historical time moves irreversibly forwards. Moreover, it reflects external shocks to the system which change, in ways not easily analyzed by the use of purely deductive methods, the path that will henceforth be followed. In the context of a historical process that has no long-run equilibrium position to which it is tending, what is the meaning or sense of "general equilibrium" *à la* Walras?

Thus post-Keynesians, like many mainstream economists, have abandoned general equilibrium analysis for Marshall's partial equilibrium framework, with emphasis on the events of the disequilibrium adjustment process. With regard to money, post-Keynesians reject the neoclassical comparative-static proposition that money is neutral, in the sense that an exogenous change in its quantity, once all adjustments have run their course, produces a proportional change in all prices, leaving real phenomena unchanged. Rather they focus on the events of the transitional period, in which the world is continually enmeshed, during which a change in the supply of money may have powerful real effects on output and employment.

Money, prices, and wages in an uncertain world

A central question for monetary theory is why people hold money, which yields no interest, rather than interest-bearing financial assets or service-providing tangible physical goods. Clearly money, like tangible assets, yields implicit services-in-kind. The nature of these services must lie in the uncertainties associated with the process of historical time. An indication of their magnitude may be found in the fact that money continues to be held and used even in countries where the annual rate of inflation (the inflation tax) approaches triple-digit figures.

Keynes recognized that in a world of uncertainty moving through calendar time, money serves as a mechanism for deferring decisions and avoiding commitment. In order for money to serve as a means of payment, supply and demand contracts must be denominated in money units, and such contracts must be legally enforceable. Money buys goods in these markets, and goods buy money, but goods with few exceptions never buy goods. Effective demand thus involves wants plus the ability to pay, and therein lies the importance of financial conditions for the real world. Modern money can function as the medium of exchange only because the community knows the state will enforce all contracts specified in terms of legal tender, that is, some national currency established by the state.

In a world of historical uncertainty in which production takes place over time, the existence of money and wage contracts permits some sharing of the burden of uncertainty. It is the uncertainty inherent in historical time, rather than the lack of synchronization between expenses incurred and payments received, that is necessary and sufficient for the existence of money. In a world of perfect certainty, in which the price of everything was known, all goods would be perfectly liquid, and there would be no need for a special money asset.

Production takes time, and this implies that a good today is a different economic quantity from the physically identical good tomorrow. Whenever resources are to be committed to produce a flow of goods for a delivery date in the future, the commitments inevitably are tied to a supply price, based on the expected future costs of production. Underlying this supply price of produced goods is the fundamental relationship between the money wage rate and average labor productivity that governs per unit labor costs. As Keynes insisted (1936), it is the expectation of stable, that is, sticky, money wage rates that encourages the public to hold money as a temporary abode of purchasing power. For if money wage rates, and with them the price level, were expected to rise precipitously, the public would be unwilling to hold its wealth in the form of a depreciating stock of money. Sticky money wage rates, which do not adjust in the short run to changes in aggregate demand, are thus a necessary condition for money to serve its other critical function as a store of value.

From the viewpoint of monetary theory, the crucial assumption that vitiates the orthodox type of analysis is the stipulation that labor markets clear like other markets, with demand determined by marginal productivity and supply governed by the real wage labor can command. This, in effect, imposes full employment by assumption—money in the long run can then affect only the general price and wage level. The unique importance of the price of labor—the money wage—is not acknowledged, but instead is treated simply as one price among the many prices determining the general equilibrium of the system.

Post-Keynesians view money wages as determined in the short run not primarily by market forces of supply and demand as is the price of peanuts and other commodities, but rather as a result of an administered price process between employers and employees, where both explicit and implicit labor contracts are first set up and then actually prevail over some future period. The implicit components are important because, unlike capital or land, workers are human beings whose output is affected by their feelings, attitudes, and morale. As a result, labor as a factor of production is unique. Its productivity is not independent of the wage which it is paid. Money wages are inflexible downwards because if the implicit contract is abrogated and wages are reduced in the face of excess supply, workers will become resentful, their productivity will fall, and the employer will acquire a bad reputation. These implicit contracts are the reason why the concept of the "just wage" is still meaningful in labor negotiations.

It follows that, if money wages can be regarded as exogeneously predetermined in this manner in the short run, prices must adjust to money wages rather than the converse. It is thus real wages which are determined endogenously by market forces. In this view, the price level (or rate of inflation) becomes resolved only after the money wage (or rate of money wage increase) has been determined. More orthodox theorists argue, in contrast, that relative prices, with money wages being merely one such price, are ground out as solutions to the set of simultaneous equations that describe the system's behavior. Not surprisingly, in such a model, monetary change in the long run can only affect the absolute price level. In contrast, in a post-Keynesian world, money can affect real and nominal variables in both the short and the long run.

An endogenous money stock

Insofar as money itself is concerned, perhaps the most fundamental point of difference between post-Keynesians and mainstream economists concerns their views as to how the stock of money comes into being. Post-Keynesians, in sharp contrast to monetarists, regard the stock of money as being essentially endogenous, responding and accommodating to changes in the level of money wages. In the *Treatise* (1930), Keynes insisted that money "comes into existence along with debts"—in other words, that the supply of money is related to production contracts and any debts which they necessitate. Money does not enter the system like manna from heaven—or from the sky via Milton Friedman's helicopter. Nor is it simply the creature of the central bank's policies. The central bank determines the stock of legal tender, or what is called the high-powered money base. The public decides the amount of legal tender it wishes to deposit with the banking system and other near-bank financial intermediaries, and the banks decide the amount they wish to maintain as cash reserves and the amount they wish to hold as earning assets. Conventional analysis assumes that because these ratios are stable, the money stock is exogenous. This point of view ignores completely the historical fact that the purpose of central banks has been to accommodate the stock of money to changes in the needs for trade. *Post-Keynesians rank the supportive responsibilities of central banks above their control duties.*

Production takes time, as already noted. In modern economies, production costs are normally incurred and paid prior to receiving any sales revenues. Of course, if current production costs simply duplicate those from the preceding period, then the present proceeds from past production and sales can be used to finance current costs. But in general, apart from the fantasy of the stationary state, this is not the way the world behaves. Wage increases raise business production costs. Even if production and sales continue at an unchanged pace, businesses will then require more working capital to finance their now higher-valued inventories of goods-in-process. Unless they are able to run down their liquid assets, they will have to increase their borrowing from their banks. Business firms thus borrow in expectation of future sales revenue to finance higher current production costs. It is this endogenous nature of the money supply process that explains the observed close statistical correlation between changes in the rate of change of the money stock and changes in the level of money income.

While post-Keynesian economists tend to regard the nominal money stock as endogenously governed by money wage levels, they differ again from monetarists in treating the process of money creation, that is, the asset side of bank balance sheets, as significant. It is often said that the heart of any economic system lies in its credit structure. It makes a difference whether banks purchase newly created financial assets (lending to finance deficit expenditure) or whether they simply purchase already existing financial assets (altering the liquidity composition of wealth portfolios).

This leads post-Keynesians to focus on the credit side of bank intermediation, in contrast with monetarists who argue that it is some variant of the money stock which is the critical variable. When banks purchase a previously existing financial asset (marketable security), the effect is to change the composition of the private sector's wealth portfolio, but to leave its total assets unchanged. When banks grant loans (purchase a newly created nonmarketable security), the effect is to change the total assets and total liabilities of the private sector. In the first case there is no monetization of a newly issued debt; in the second case there is.

Finance and investment behavior

Post-Keynesians view business cycles, economic growth, and the factoral distribution of income as being jointly governed by the same key determinant—the rate of investment. Rather than conceiving investment as being governed by saving, as in the orthodox neoclassical model, post-Keynesians follow Michal Kalecki (1966) in arguing that investment in part generates the profits necessary to finance itself. In modern capitalist economies the funds for investment are obtained largely out of internal cash flows—that is, depreciation charges and retained earnings. Still, not all the funds are obtained internally. Thus, post-Keynesian analysis further emphasizes the fundamental role played by advanced credit instruments and institutions in the investment process that characterizes developed capitalist economies.

While the conventional analysis emphasizes the importance of the expected return in determining the amount of investment that will be undertaken, this expected return is not easily ascertained in the real world where the future is inherently unknowable. This leads to the importance of what Keynes (1936) called "animal spirits" in the investment process, and the independence of investment from saving decisions. If businessmen wish to invest, and bankers will accommodate their demands for credit, it is investment that determines saving rather than the reverse. The endogenous nature of the money stock, meanwhile, permits investment expenditures to be carried out independently of current savings flows.

In modern capitalist economies it is impossible to construct a theory of investment that is independent of the portfolio preferences of businessmen and financial managers. A decision to invest necessarily implies simultaneously a decision to acquire a tangible asset and to issue a financial asset. Since the future is essentially unknowable, and yet decisions with long-run implications nevertheless must be undertaken, real world businessmen are forced to rely on conventions. Past experience is widely believed to be the common basis for determining attitudes and responses to uncertainty and risk, and so it is for the evaluation of the uncertain prospects which attend financial values and investment decisions. This is reflected not only in changing stock market values, but also in the changing asset and liability structures of firm and household balance sheets. The ratio of debt servicing charges to net profits, leverage (debt to equity) ratios, and the term structure of private debts all reflect the views of businessmen and bankers as to what is permissible, and these standards of permissiveness change systematically in response to past experience.

As one result, capitalist economies give rise to a growth process which is inherently cyclical. During prosperity, firms are induced to borrow and increase their debt ratios to finance new capital expenditures. As long as the expansion proceeds, the leaders in this process are rewarded by greater profits. Gradually, the accepted (subjective) credit standards adjust, but as carrying costs and debt ratios rise, the financial structure becomes (objectively) increasingly precarious and fragile. Eventually a downturn in business activity is severe enough to impair confidence, credit standards are raised, and a liquidity panic will, unless offset by government deficits and central bank accommodation, lead to a general decline in asset values. In this way, the stability and prosperity of an expansion breeds the instability and collapse of the crisis.

As stated, post-Keynesians do not regard it as useful to view the economy as moving along some balanced secular growth path, around which exogenous shocks cause cyclical fluctuations which are then dampened by self-correcting market forces. Balanced growth is inconsistent with the very existence of financial assets in an uncertain world moving inexorably through historical time. They rather share the Marxist view that business cycles are an inherent aspect of real world capitalist systems, the result of a failure to coordinate economic activity from without. It is this lack of planning which leads to disproportions and mismatches in production and consumption. Crises can be viewed as serving a functional role, helping to solve the problems of accumulation that become acute during the expansion phases of the capitalist business cycle.

There are several distinct Marxist crisis theories. Nevertheless, put most crudely in Marxist terms, the post-Keynesian argument runs as follows. During booms, the working classes gain strength as full employment is approached, and workers use this enhanced power to obtain higher money wages and better working conditions. They are also able to change jobs more frequently, to prevent speedups by employers, and to take life a little easier. By so doing, they make life less enjoyable for the class owning and controlling capital goods and organizing the production process. An economic crisis, by producing unemployment, serves to restore the profit conditions necessary for the continuation of the capital accumulation process. Each crisis solves its own particular problems, but the solutions always generate new problems, which then require still further solutions. It is in this sense that post-Keynesian economics can legitimately be viewed as having a significant post-Marxian component. Nevertheless, while Marxist and post-Keynesian arguments run parallel in this regard, there are important differences and the two should not be confused. Post-Keynesian economists generally avoid those aspects of Marxist theory which are either metaphysical or ideological. Post-Keynesians are not in general wedded to the dialectical process, and like other "vulgar" economists have little to say about such concepts as class struggle, alienation, or exploitation.

While economic crises always produce unemployment, in recent years they have also been accompanied by inflation. The recent world inflation is widely regarded as having begun in the United States as a response to excess demand growing out of deficit-financed war expenditures for Vietnam. This inflation was propelled onward and outward by synchronous booms throughout the capitalist countries which greatly augmented aggregate demand for world resources. The prolonged boom of the 1960s and the demand-pull inflation that it created in turn produced cost-push pressures which have persisted into the world recession of the 1970s, and account for the current state of stagflation. Inflation now coexists with unemployment mainly because the working classes have gained and retained sufficient political and economic strength to battle more evenly with capital over shares of the national income.

The causes of inflation

The contemporary orthodox division of economics into two parts, microeconomics and macroeconomics, grew out of the earlier Marshallian division of the subject into the theory of value and the theory of money. In microeconomics, supply and demand interact to determine relative prices through the application of either Marshallian partial-equilibrium or Walrasian general-equilibrium analysis. Modern macroeconomics, in the version that has come to be identified as the "neoclassical synthesis," lumps together the old quantity theory of money, which determines the level of absolute prices, with a bastardized version of Keynes centering on how price rigidities may prevent the economy from actually reaching full-employment equilibrium.

For modern post-Keynesians, in contrast, the rate of inflation is determined primarily by the rate of increase of nominal money wages relative to labor productivity. Over wide sectors of the economy, prices are largely cost-determined, based on a mark-up over unit labor costs. (The main exceptions are the agricultural and raw materials sectors where prices are still jointly determined by supply and demand.) This mark-up of prices over unit labor costs will be constant over time for the economy as a whole so long as the capital and labor shares of national income are constant, irrespective of the assumptions governing price-setting behavior. So long as factor shares are constant, a constant mark-up will result even if all markets are assumed perfectly competitive and the neoclassical assumption made that all factors are paid the value of their marginal products. A rise in raw material prices, a rise in the share of national income going to government, and an increase in the rate of investment expenditures will all tend to lead to a higher mark-up, reducing real wages by driving a larger wedge between unit wage costs and prices.

As stated above, once wage contracts have been negotiated, the price level or the rate of inflation is largely a predetermined variable. To the extent labor is able to build the expected rate of inflation into its wage settlements, the ensuing rate of inflation will be governed by the extent to which money wage rates have risen more rapidly than average labor productivity.

How is this position to be reconciled with the abundant empirical evidence that major historical increases and decreases in the rate of inflation are accompanied by increases and decreases in the rate of growth of the money stock? Post-Keynesians maintain that the high-powered monetary base as determined by the central bank, while admittedly exogenous in the control sense, is endogenous in the real world and hence in the statistical sense.

This accommodation process may be readily explained as follows. Over the longer run, *assuming considerations of variable velocity can be safely ignored*, the growth of demand for money can be represented tautologically as:

$$(1) \qquad \dot{M} = \dot{p} + \dot{y}$$

where M is the demand for the nominal money stock, p is the price level, y is real output, and the superscript $\cdot$ indicates the rate of growth of the corresponding variable. Monetarists then assume that the growth of real income can be treated as if it followed a steady trend, and the money market continually cleared. If these assumptions are accepted, the monetarist conclusion emerges that the proximate determinant of the rate of inflation is the rate by which the nominal money stock increases in excess of the growth of real output.

$$(2) \qquad \dot{p} = \dot{M} - \dot{y}$$

From this follows Friedman's famous rule (Friedman, 1969) that in order to ensure price stability the nominal money stock should be increased at a constant 3 to 5 percent per year, to allow for the 3 to 5 percent increase per year in the level of real economic activity ($\dot{y}$).

The post-Keynesian view is that the rate of inflation is governed by the extent that nominal wage increases exceed the rate of growth of average labor productivity. This may similarly be written tautologically:

$$(3) \qquad \dot{w} \equiv \dot{W} - \dot{p}$$

where W is the average level of nominal money wages, w is the average real wage, and the superscript $\cdot$ again denotes the rate of growth of the corresponding variable. Over the long run the rate of growth of real wages, which depends on the growth of labor productivity, the ratio of import prices relative to domestic prices, the levels of indirect taxation and profit mark-ups, will also have a fairly steady trend. *Assuming that the mark-up remains constant, real wages will grow at the rate of growth of labor productivity.* The proximate determinant of inflation is then the rate at which nominal money wages rise in excess of the growth of average labor productivity. To the extent money wages grow more rapidly than the growth of labor productivity, unit labor costs and therefore the price level will rise accordingly, as follows:

$$(4) \qquad\qquad \dot{p} = \dot{W} - \dot{z}$$

where $\dot{z}$ is the rate of growth of average labor productivity.

If both the level and rate of change of wages and prices are predetermined and inflexible downwards, equations (1) and (4) taken together imply that if the monetary authorities do not permit the nominal money stock to accommodate to the rate of increase of money wages, aggregate demand will not be sufficient to maintain the secular growth of real output. As a result there will be downward pressure on the growth of real income $\dot{y}$, a rise in interest rates, and an accompanying rise in unemployment rates.

The critical post-Keynesian assumption is that the mark-up and so labor's share is approximately given in the short run. On this assumption, the endogenous nature of the money stock in the postwar period is readily explained. To the extent that the monetary authorities follow an accommodating monetary policy, permitting credit to respond to "reasonable" demands so as to avoid any undesired rise in unemployment and interest rates, the rate of growth of the nominal money stock will be determined by the past rate of growth of money wages.

This position is substantiated empirically. Both the money stock and the high-powered money base, at least for the United States, Canada, and the United Kingdom, are highly correlated over the postwar period with the past rate of change of money wage rates. Both a Keynesian demand inflation generated by spurts in investment or government expenditures, and a cost inflation generated by increases in wage or profit demands, have to be, and consequently are, validated by the monetary authorities. This is a practical, and not a logical, necessity.

Monetary authorities are thus caught in a terrible dilemma. They can fulfill their obligation to resist depreciation of the monetary unit and protect fixed-income wealth-owners by abandoning their government's commitment to full employment, and permitting the unemployment rate to rise. But their overriding short-term commitment—in fact their very *raison d'etre*—is to a stable and healthy financial system. It is this which induces them to make the reserves available to support all reasonable demands for credit, since the alternative would be financial chaos, spiraling interest rates, and a wave of bankrupt firms.

Some policy implications

As Keynes argued, economics is essentially a moral and not a natural science. It employs introspection and value judgments. Once there are major disparities in income distribution within a country, or among countries, the market mechanism ceases to function equitably, since it is weighted heavily in favor of the purchasing power the rich command. It is, for example, now increasingly recognized in the development literature that economic growth does not automatically filter down to the poorest sections of a society.

One of the ways in which the market system systematically discriminates against the poor is the way in which it allocates the new credit associated with a growing money stock. Access to credit is valuable, yet within any capitalist country, the poor receive proportionately little credit. Since they do not possess the collateral to guarantee loans, they are excluded by the market from the benefits of new credit. The same exclusion of the poor occurs at the international level. The Third World, with 70 percent of the world's population, received less than 5 percent of the international reserves created during 1970-75. If a more equitable system of providing credit is to be established, an international Central Bank with the power to create an international currency must be set up, and the access to its facilities based not on past affluence but rather on future growth needs and potential. Similarly, within a national system, the poor should be entitled to receive at least a *pro rata* share in new credit creation, and be able to market these entitlements.

Another policy implication of the post-Keynesian paradigm is the necessity of some form of social planning to resolve the problem of stagflation in modern capitalist economies. If price increases are generated by rising unit costs, the result of money wage rates increasing more rapidly than average labor productivity, then inflation cannot be countered effectively by conventional fiscal or monetary demand management policies. A restriction of aggregate demand growth, engineered for example by more restrictive fiscal and monetary policy, would result, not in a fall in inflation, but rather in a fall in real output and a rise in interest rates and unemployment.

Conventional policy medicine, including Friedman's famous rule, could in principle work, but at such a tremendous cost in forgone real output and employment, and with such a terrible punishment of innocent and weaker parties, as to be politically unacceptable. There is, it must be conceded, some level of unemployment at which workers, irrespective of experienced past and expected future rates of inflation, could be cowed into accepting money wage increases no greater than the rate of growth of labor productivity, so that unit labor costs would remain stable. But given the current widespread perception that governments (and their central banks) have both the ability and responsibility to prevent mass unemployment, such unemployment rates would not permit a democratically elected government to survive the next election.

Consequently, almost all post-Keynesian economists lean toward some type of incomes policy as the only feasible solution to the problem of stagflation. The chief problem with incomes policies, as is by now well known, is that no capitalist government has yet succeeded in devising one that will work over the long haul. Government-imposed wage and price controls necessarily interfere with market allocation processes, and the resulting distortions rise exponentially the longer controls are maintained.

Perhaps the central political difficulty is that all stabilization policies have strong distributional implications. In the case of an incomes policy, this distributional aspect is made more explicit. As long as efforts to improve relative incomes take the form of increases in money wages, decentralized collective bargaining has a strong tendency to lead to inflation in all economies where the government accepts some responsibility for full employment. (The only recent exceptions are Switzerland and Germany, both countries where the costs of unemployment can be shifted to foreign workers, reducing the political pressure on their monetary authorities to validate excessive wage increases. In the case of Germany the presence in the collective consciousness of two hyperinflations, during which all monetary values were completely eroded, has undoubtedly served both to moderate money wage demands and to shift the government's unemployment inflation policy trade-off towards a lower target rate of inflation. In the case of Switzerland the country's role as international banker has served the same functions.)

The alternative to such collective bargaining is the development of an acceptable policy on relative incomes—not only among wage-earners, but also between the recipients of wage and nonwage income. If the government is forced to put itself in the position of regulating wage increases, it will soon be pushed into taking a position not only on appropriate life-cycle income profiles, but also on appropriate relative wage structures among occupations. From there it is but a short step to specifying the appropriate incomes for rentiers and entrepreneurs, and the very foundations of the system will be fundamentally challenged. In order for a modern capitalist system with collective bargaining to avoid stagflation, it becomes necessary to achieve a consensus about equitable relative incomes—and it is precisely this which seems beyond our present political competence.

There is, however, one possible way out. When private decisions impose external costs on others, it is widely accepted that the government is justified in imposing a tax price, to force decision-makers to internalize these costs. For example, economists have long favored using the market system rather than controls to restrain pollution. A similar argument has recently been applied by some post-Keynesians to stagflation. Since money wage increases in excess of productivity gains cause unit labor costs and therefore prices to rise, they may be thought of as being analogous to pollution. If corporations wish to negotiate labor contracts that raise wages by say, 10 percent, this is a free country and so let them—without price or wage controls. But because they are imposing an inflation cost on the rest of us, they should be asked to pay a tax on that part of the wage bill that exceeds the reduction in costs from increased labor productivity. In that way, they may be dissuaded from increasing wages beyond the noninflationary rate of growth of labor productivity. Such a "Tax-Based Incomes Policy" could also be applied as a carrot. Firms which grant wage increases and price increases lower than a stipulated amount could receive a subsidy bonus.

If effective, such a policy would tend to freeze the *status quo* of the existing distribution of income among workers, and between labor and capital. As a result it is particularly difficult to choose an appropriate stage of the business cycle to implement it. Wages are a poor control variable, and the problem of wage drift would undoubtedly necessitate a further extension of government bureaucratic power into the marketplace. The wage level as such cannot be directly managed by government action, but manipulated only indirectly by operating on wages in individual industries and occupations. There is simply no good substitute for real competition in labor and product markets.

Nevertheless, such a policy does follow from the logic of the post-Keynesian analysis. While it is not the only policy which can be derived from that analysis, and many post-Keynesians maintain that an effective incomes policy can only emerge out of a more comprehensive system of indicative planning, it would appear to be the route which comes closest to being politically feasible at present. Most important, it has a better chance of moving public policy along more constructive lines than the orthodox policy recommendations.

Continuing and possibly increasing wage inflation—the *status quo*. A slump and a massive rise in unemployment to keep money wage increases low. Or some form of incomes policy. These three alternatives exhaust the set. There are no other games in town.

JOHN B. BURBIDGE

The International Dimension

No formal post-Keynesian treatment of international trade
has yet appeared that would correspond to the orthodox,
neoclassical theory of trade. Nonetheless, in the work of Joan
Robinson, Michal Kalecki, Nicholas Kaldor, and other post-
Keynesian writers, building on Keynes' *General Theory* and
the elements of classical theory emphasized by Piero Sraffa,
one can discern the main outline of an alternative to the
prevailing theory of international trade. While the details of
this outline still need to be filled in, the outline itself is
sufficient to indicate the form which the post-Keynesian
theory of international trade, as it is further developed, is
likely to take. This essay, after first indicating some of the
salient features of the alternative post-Keynesian approach,
will then compare it with the orthodox, neoclassical model of
trade, showing how it may lead to a different set of policy
conclusions.

Two themes in post-Keynesian theory

Two themes which permeate the post-Keynesian literature
are that the social relations of production—part of what
Marx termed "the mode of production"—and historical time
must be taken seriously. These themes carry over directly

into the study of international trade. Differences in the assumed modes of production partly account for the differences between the two trade models which can be gleaned from post-Keynesian literature. One of these models analyzes trade among advanced capitalist economies and the other analyzes trade between a capitalist economy and an economy producing some primary product, like food, with an artisan mode of production. Each of these models will be further elaborated below.

The other theme, the theme that historical time must be taken seriously, has a great impact on the nature of the model, whichever it is that one considers appropriate. In *The General Theory* (1936) Keynes showed that much of what happens in an actual economy can be understood only by assuming the existence of uncertainty. The essence of a real economy that operates in historical time is that its past cannot be changed and its future cannot be known. In such an economy, there may be no tendency to move towards long-run equilibrium. Indeed, one may go further and say that it is difficult to conceive of what "equilibrium" would mean in the context of an *historical process* that has no long-run position to which it is moving. These two themes also dominate the differences between the post-Keynesian and the neoclassical approaches to international trade.

Trade among developed countries

The first trade model to be taken up under the post-Keynesian rubric is the one based on Kalecki's work (1976). It is concerned with analyzing trade among advanced capitalist economies. This model relies heavily on Marx's conception of a capitalist mode of production. In the sphere of production, the capitalist-entrepreneurs run the firms—they hire and fire labor, set the wage rate, make the production and pricing decisions, and determine the level of investment. In this model, the firm is the central institution. Rentier capitalists provide the firm with finance, and workers operate the means of production. In the sphere of distribution (or circulation), there are two types of households—those of the capitalists and those of the workers. The capitalists are wealthy, and thus their consumption is not limited by their current income. The workers, in contrast, are relatively poor, and Kalecki assumes that they consume all of their current income.

In any particular short period, the actual level of investment undertaken by the firms is determined, in the model, by decisions taken in earlier periods. Over a sequence of short periods, the level of investment decisions depends on a complex set of factors—historical, political, psychological, as well as the economic factors which Keynes (1936) (and Joan Robinson following him) summarized as the "animal spirits" of the entrepreneurs. The model is a monetary one in that the future cannot be known, and therefore money is required to link the present with the future. Entrepreneurs tend to be dominated by current experience. When profits are high, they undertake additional investment in the expectation that these high profits will continue, and vice versa. The higher level of investment implies higher profits, leading to still higher levels of investment until the capital stock has been expanded to the point where the increasing supply overwhelms the growth of demand. At that point, sales, profits, and investment all fall off, resulting in a period of cumulative decline. The process may be reversed by the need to replace the capital stock. In any event, business cycles of boom and bust are the normal state of affairs.

What happens when we introduce international trade into a world of such manufacturing nations? From the point of view of one nation, exports tend to increase employment, output, and profits; imports tend to reduce them. The pattern of trade that emerges, for a given set of exchange rates, depends on the ratio of average hourly earnings to average la-

141

bor productivity (direct costs per unit of output) across the countries, measured, say, in U.S. dollars (cost) per unit of output. The countries which have the lowest unit costs tend to develop a surplus on current account in the balance of payments since they are able to undercut other countries in foreign markets. This increases their profits and output. The higher levels of profits, in turn, provide the finance to expand capacity and install still more efficient equipment, which tends to make their competitive advantage all the stronger. By contrast, the countries which are relatively less efficient are likely to experience high unemployment and low profits, and therefore tend to fall further behind in the competitive struggle for markets. As Robinson (1973) says in describing the "new mercantilism" that then emerges to guide public policy, "Every industrial country wants a surplus on income account. 'Export led growth' is the most convenient way of running modern capitalism. Who succeeds at any moment is accidental, largely depending upon historical circumstances and political and psychological influences. Success leads to success and failure engenders failure."

Working with a similar model, John Cornwall (1978) has come to similar conclusions. "[T]he factors that lead to imaginative and successful export drives are the same factors that spur growth rates for the whole economy. . . . [T]he neotechnology theory of international trade. . . , with its emphasis on differences across countries in technologies, on the importance of scale economies, borrowed technology and R and D, the quality of entrepreneurship and investment outlays, is the most adequate theory explaining export patterns and success."

It is worth noting that the process mentioned above may exist even with flexible exchange rates. Consider the situation in which a country is falling behind in the competitive struggle and is therefore borrowing from abroad to cover the deficit on current account in its balance of payments. The deficit is likely, under flexible exchange rates, to cause a devaluation of the country's currency. But this will tend to raise the prices of imported goods relative to the prices of domestically produced goods, particularly if the prices of the imported goods are fixed in terms of the currency of one of the efficient, balance-of-payments-surplus nations like West Germany or Japan. If the imported goods figure prominently in workers' consumption, then this result will set the stage for what John Hicks (1965) calls "real wage resistance"—resistance by workers to cuts in the purchasing power of their money wages. The workers strike, foreign contracts are lost, wages and unit costs measured in U.S. dollars rise and the country is no better off—indeed the country may well be worse off than before devaluation. Recent economic history in the United Kingdom appears to fit this case nicely.

The firms in the countries which have a surplus on current account will have, on average, substantial profits to invest abroad. The process by which the United States bought up Canadian industry and Japan is now buying up Australian industry is well known. Whether this is a good bargain or not for the deficit countries depends on what is done with the finance. Two problems faced by an economy dominated by the foreign branch plants of international firms are that: (a) its exports tend to be lower than they would otherwise be because one plant of an international firm does not compete with other plants of the same company in other countries; and (b) unit costs tend to be higher, and thus consumers pay higher prices, because plants are likely to be run well below capacity output. The two problems are obviously related.

With the continuation of the foreign investment process for several decades, it becomes clear that a few international firms will eventually grow into exceedingly large corporations, whose powers rival and may even exceed those of national governments. The emphasis on the role and the behavior of the firm in the post-Keynesian model of international trade seems to be well justified in the light of recent economic history.

Trade between developed and less developed countries

The other kind of post-Keynesian trade model is one in which countries with two different modes of production trade with one another. Of course, this type of situation could occur, and in fact often does occur, within a single nation; but there is much to be learned about the economic history of international trade by applying such a model to different nations.

This model is also based on Kalecki's work. In 1943 Kalecki distinguished "cost-determined" prices, such as the prices of manufactured goods, from "demand-determined" prices, such as those of raw materials and agricultural products. Let us focus on agricultural production here. The main reason for the difference between the price behavior of manufactured goods and that of agricultural products is that the supply of manufactured goods tends to be elastic, the firms being quite happy to supply more output at a constant price, while the supply of agricultural products tends to be inelastic, at least in the short period. The mode of production for manufacturing is assumed to be capitalistic, and the mode of production for the agricultural sector is assumed to be like that of an artisan economy. Each family owns land and certain implements of production, producing an output which is then sold in a competitive market. What are the implications of this model for international trade?

Kaldor (1976) has used the model to discuss a wide range of long-period phenomena observable from recent international experience, even though the model has its roots in the development models of the Physiocrats and the English classical economists. If one assumes that labor productivity grows more quickly in agriculture than in manufacturing, the model predicts that there will be a tendency for the prices of agricultural goods to fall relative to prices of manufactured goods. Since the demand for food tends to be inelastic, agricultural incomes will be lowered and there will be a movement of labor from rural areas to the cities. The facts of economic history are consistent with this story.

Kaldor has recently used the model, in a short-period context, to show how crop failures may lead to severe inflation and recession in the manufacturing centers. A crop failure pushes up the relative price of agricultural goods, which, on the assumption that the demand for food is inelastic, causes an increase in agricultural incomes. If the farmers save part of their higher incomes, there will be a decline in demand for manufactured goods, because manufacturing workers are now forced to spend more on food and have less left to spend on manufactured goods. Employment, output, and profits in manufacturing all fall. If the manufacturing workers resist the decrease in their real wages by seeking and obtaining increases in money-wage rates, the prices of manufactured goods will rise and the change in relative prices between agriculture and manufacturing will tend to be offset. Movements in the terms of trade which should redress the imbalance between the two trading regions may simply cause inflation and unemployment. As Kaldor says, ". . .the emergence of shortages which should accelerate the growth of availabilities of primary products through improvements in the terms of trade may lead instead to an inflation of manufacturers' prices which tends to offset the improvement in terms of trade, and by its dampening effect on industrial activity, worsens the climate for new investment in both the primary sector and the industrial sector." Sidney Dell's recent article (1977) on Kalecki's work for the United Nations from 1946 to 1954, work in which he used two-sector models to analyze the problems of less developed countries, indicates that Kalecki arrived at similar conclusions.

The orthodox theory

How are these post-Keynesian models related to the neoclassical approach to international trade?

The modern neoclassical theory of international trade parallels the neoclassical theory of a closed economy. To understand this theory, one must examine its origins. Prior to the publication of Keynes' *The General Theory*, the study of economics was divided into two parts: the theory of value (or relative prices) and the theory of money. Alfred Marshall's *Principles of Economics* held that demand and supply determine *relative* values, or prices, given the assumption of full employment of all resources. The quantity theory of money, with the stock of money as the key determinant, was then introduced to explain the level of *absolute* prices. In *The General Theory*, Keynes held this to be a false division of the subject, but his point that the theory of value and distribution would have to be adapted to a monetary economy in which the future cannot be known and the past cannot be changed, was not taken seriously. In the reconstruction of economics after World War II, the subject was again divided into two parts: microeconomics and macroeconomics. Microeconomics combines Marshall's partial-equilibrium analysis with Walras' general-equilibrium analysis. Macroeconomics, on the other hand, lumps Hicks' (1937) interpretation of Keynes with the old quantity theory of money. The two parts taken together, the microeconomic and the macroeconomic, constitute the "neoclassical synthesis." The incompatibility between the parts is glossed over. The microeconomic theory assumes wage and price flexibility so that a full-employment equilibrium is assured, while the macroeconomic theory explains why the economy may be at less than full employment equilibrium for some time because of rigidities—that is, it discusses the short-term deviation of the economy from the full-employment path and the process of adjusting from one position of long-run equilibrium to another. Consistency between the two parts is maintained only by omitting the main difference between Keynes and his predecessors—the role of uncertainty and of money in an actual economy.

The above outline also describes the neoclassical theory of international trade. This theory is also divided into two main branches—the "pure theory of international trade," which is microeconomic, and the "monetary" theory of international trade or, as it is sometimes called, "international finance," which is macroeconomic.

In the former it is assumed that wage and price flexibility guarantees full employment of resources. Here the model used most frequently is the Heckscher-Ohlin one, which is simply the two-sector (or two-output) general-equilibrium model as it has been applied to international trade by Harry Johnson (1958, 1962), James Meade (1952, 1955), and others. This model, like other general-equilibrium, microeconomic models, simply assumes away all the questions that Keynes thought to be interesting. The main development in this area has been the gradual shift from a partial-equilibrium, Marshallian type of analysis to a general-equilibrium type of analysis.

As far as the monetary aspect of international trade is concerned, there has been a significant shift in emphasis over just the past thirty years. Prior to Keynes, Hume's quantity theory of money adjustment model—the "price-specie flow mechanism"—was used to show how a deficit in the balance of trade would induce a capital outflow, and this in turn would lead to a fall in the domestic price level relative to foreign prices, thus restoring equilibrium in the balance of payments. Attempts to integrate Keynes' analysis of income adjustments into the analysis of the international payments

John B. Burbidge

mechanism has proven difficult, and this, in turn, has led to a long controversy as to the process of adjustment to "equilibrium" in the balance of payments. As Richard Cooper notes in his introduction to *International Finance* (1974), ". . .international monetary economics. . .shares the difficulties arising from the failure, so far, to integrate monetary theory into the main corpus of economic theory in a meaningful and practically relevant way."

To summarize, then, one can see that there are significant differences between either of the two post-Keynesian trade models and the more orthodox approach to international trade theory. The post-Keynesian models are not normally in long-run equilibrium, the neoclassical models are. The former attempts to tell a causal, sequential story of how a particular historical process unfolds, the other does not. Institutions and the concept of a mode of production have a major impact on the results of the post-Keynesian theory, while the neoclassical model is so free of institutions that it is assumed to apply to all kinds of human societies. The monetary segment of the orthodox theory is closer to the post-Keynesian approach in that it incorporates elements of *The General Theory*, but there are still major differences. These differences are primarily the differences between neoclassical macroeconomics and post-Keynesian macroeconomics.

Policy implications

As noted in the introduction, the post-Keynesian theory of international trade is not well developed and thus neither are its policy implications. One may, however, at some risk, draw policy implications out of the post-Keynesian approach. The theme that emerges is that the problems in international trade are more difficult to solve than orthodox theory would lead one to believe.

One implication of the above discussion of trade between

148

developed capitalist economies is that neither fixed nor flexible exchange rates may be able to solve the balance of payments problems of those countries which are falling behind in the competitive struggle for markets. If there is "real-wage resistance," as Hicks suggests, then devaluation, when prices are fixed in the currencies of the balance-of-payments-surplus countries, will lead to an increase in domestic prices, and this, in turn, will lead to pressure for higher money-wage rates. The resulting inflation will make the domestic country less competitive internationally and the balance of payments deficit larger.

In this situation, certain post-Keynesian writers have argued for some form of incomes policy in order to bring the costs of production under control. When wages are controlled and there is a devaluation of the domestic currency, prices in terms of the domestic currency will increase and real wages will fall. Recent economic history indicates that workers will react strongly against such policies. The subsequent strikes and work slowdowns may result in the loss of foreign contracts and a further worsening of the balance of payments deficit. Some have suggested that perhaps a combination of instruments can be used to achieve, simultaneously, a solution to the problems of balance of payments deficits, unemployment, and inflation. Kalecki's analysis, however, leads one to be pessimistic about the prospects for finding such a combination.

Another implication of the "new mercantilism" which permeates international trade policy is that prospects for free trade, which many believe would eliminate inefficient production and increase world output, are not good. While it may be collectively in the interest of nations to have free trade, the competitive struggle for markets amongst countries, in which countries act in their own self-interest, makes it unlikely that free trade will ever be fully realized.

That individuals acting in their own self-interest may not

advance the welfare of all is a recurrent theme in the work of Joan Robinson and Kalecki, but the flaw in the neoclassical case for the free market was noted long ago by Tibor Scitovsky (1942). He showed that in a competitive market, while it appears to be in the interests of buyers to form a combine to turn the terms of trade in their favor (the same applies to the sellers), the process of turning a competitive market into a bilateral monopoly can easily lead to everyone being worse off. To reverse the process is difficult, as the recent negotiations in Geneva prove.

An implication which can be deduced from a model where a manufactured-goods producer trades with a primary-products producer is that liberalization of trade is unlikely to improve the relative position of the less developed countries, which tend to produce primary products. As Kaldor suggested in his Presidential Address to the Royal Economic Society (1976), events which force up the prices of primary products relative to manufactured goods will do so only temporarily. Eventually the prices of manufactured goods, which are purchased by primary producers, will rise, and this will swing the distribution of income in favor of the developed countries. It would seem that, to gain ground, the less developed countries must somehow jump over the technological gap that separates them from the more developed countries and set up their own manufacturing sectors.

PAUL DAVIDSON

Natural Resources

Post-Keynesian theorists view the economic problems surrounding raw materials (that is, natural resources) in a very
different light from orthodox neoclassical economic theorists.
This point can perhaps best be illustrated in the context of
the current so-called "energy crisis."

In 1973, the onset of an energy crisis, in a world that for a
century had been plagued by a potential oversupply of fossil
fuels at existing market prices, caught many knowledgeable
observers by surprise. The energy shortage immediately
generated a search for a scapegoat or a rational explanation
of the predicament faced by the highly developed capitalist
economies heavily based on energy resources, such as the
United States, Western Europe, and Japan.

Orthodox economic theory has taught that businessmen's
single-minded pursuit of profit opportunities, tempered by
competition and the absence of externalities, would result in
an optimum allocation of resources and the maximization
of the community's welfare. Thus if orthodox theory is to be
believed, executives of multinational energy companies
should not be pilloried for failing to meet the needs of any
one selfish nation, for in their pursuit of profits they are
unwittingly maximizing the economic welfare of mankind.
As for the evidence showing the lack of competition at the

various stages of the vertically integrated oil industry, some students of the industry, such as J. E. Hartshorn (1962) claim that the international supply of crude oil is "the same as what might be expected to arise from the operation of the law of comparative costs in a freely competitive international market." After all, the consumer seemed to be plentifully, and cheaply, supplied.

According to neoclassical economists, the problem of depletable natural resources such as oil is one of determining, in Robert Solow's words (1974), the "optimal social management of a stock of a nonrenewable but essential resource." An immediate consequence of this way of conceptualizing the problem is an analysis of the existing structure of the resource market to see whether it provides "proper" price allocative guidelines. If it can be proven that the market "fails," then it follows (for those who use this approach) that the role of the economist is to design policies to improve market performance and bring it closer to the competitive ideal. In other words, the first instinct of neoclassical economists in this field is to leave the decision as to the time rate of exploitation of exhaustible resources to the invisible hand, unless a market failure can be demonstrated *and* a corrective policy can be developed. Government control of prices is to be avoided.

Two fundamental questions

Post-Keynesian economic theory, however, begins at an earlier stage and raises two fundamental questions. First, can market prices, even in a competitive environment, provide adequate guidelines for approaching an efficient and optimal rate of utilization of exhaustible resources over a period of calendar time? Second, in a world of conglomerate energy companies, does rationality of entrepreneurial policies imply anticompetitive and antisocial behavior that redistributes income from consumers to producers and owners of resource-bearing property?

The "optimal" use of any exhaustible natural resource depends, in the context of private markets, on entrepreneurial decisions as to the time rate of production for that resource. For a market price system to provide guidance in determining the "optimal social management of a depletable resource" over time, *all* of the following conditions must hold:

1. Well-organized forward markets exist for each date in the future.

2. Consumers know with actuarial certainty all their needs for energy resources at each date.

3. Consumers are able and willing to exercise all these future demands by currently entering into forward contracts for each date.

4. Entrepreneurs know with actuarial certainty the cost of production associated with production flows for each date.

5. Sellers can choose between an immediate contract at today's market prices and a forward contract at the market price associated with any future delivery date (and there are over 73,000 such delivery dates in the next two centuries).

6. Entrepreneurs know with actuarial certainty the course of future interest rates.

7. The social rate of discount (the rate at which society values present over future goods) equals the rate at which entrepreneurs discount future earnings and costs.

8. No false trading occurs—that is, no production or exchange ever takes place at nonequilibrium prices.

If all these conditions are met, then, in a competitive environment, market prices can be shown to be an efficient or socially optimal way to allocate energy resources over time, in the sense of maximizing the sum of discounted consumer and producer benefits. If one or more of these conditions are violated—as they always must be in the real world—then an unfettered market system cannot provide guidance on an optimal intertemporal allocation of natural resources, and all the mumbo-jumbo of orthodox economists about the ability of "free markets" to guide "proper" decisions—as contrasted with the blunders that would be made by a bureaucracy—has no foundation in logic or in fact.

Post-Keynesian theory, on the other hand, suggests that in a world where the future is uncertain, it is impossible to identify which future intertemporal allocation path for natural resources will, in fact, be socially optimal or efficient, since the efficient or optimal path can only be defined for known future conditions. Post-Keynesian economists reject the idea that either economists or real world market prices can or do play the role of Delphic oracle. Instead, they hold that the economist's function is to analyze alternative market and regulatory controls of resource production and consumption decisions, and then to explain the implications of these alternatives for production flows, prices, income, and the distribution of wealth and economic power. Economists, it is argued, should acknowledge their role as "soft" scientists providing advice to policy-makers regarding "hard" decisions. Moreover, even as soft scientists, economists should not hesitate to suggest that policy should aim at (1) protecting consumers from paying more than the normal supply price for essential goods and services, and (2) encouraging "enterprise" and preventing "speculation" from dominating economic activities.

The role of user costs

One of the basic post-Keynesian conceptual tools for analyzing the use of natural resources is the concept of "user costs" for, as Keynes emphasized in *The General Theory* (1936), "In the case of raw materials the necessity of allowing for user cost is obvious." (Keynes borrowed the term "user cost" from Marshall but was the first to develop the concept and apply it to the question of intertemporal production from any depletable properties.) User costs constitute one of the major economic links between the current situation and the future, because they involve weighing expected future profits against current ones. The concept of user costs can be illustrated as follows.

For any particular property, the fossil fuels in the ground are a fixed inventory (or exhaustible resource). The more of these fuels that are used today, *ceteris paribus*, the less will be available for future delivery. Consequently, a rational entrepreneur will compare the present value of expected profits for a forward contract sale at each possible future date with the profitability of selling that amount today. If profit-maximizing entrepreneurs are to produce for current sale, current marginal revenue must be expected to cover not only current marginal production costs associated with that barrel of oil, but also the user costs inherent in all depletable resources—namely, the highest present value of marginal future profits given up by producing that barrel of oil currently rather than in the future. If well-organized forward markets existed in the real world, producers of natural resources could readily use the forward prices to estimate user costs. However, forward markets for oil and other natural resources for days, months, and years in the future do not exist. Only if such forward markets already existed and only if they truly represented the demand that future consumers would have (and not the views of today's speculators regarding the future demand) could entrepreneurs then employ the concept of user costs to obtain an efficient intertemporal production program by following the guidance of free market prices. Instead, the only information available to producers is the history of the industry, the current situation, and the individual's hopes, fears, and expectations about the future prices of resources. Thus the current production plans depend in large measure on unfounded expectations about the future where waves of propaganda, optimism, or pessimism can overwhelm "rational" entrepreneurs and make oil-bearing properties objects of speculation. Most ultimate consumers of oil and other natural resources do not know, nor can they predict accurately, their demands for the products of natural resources weeks, months, or years into the future.

It therefore follows that in a world where the future is uncertain, with producers "free" to make any production decisions they think most profitable, we are left with a bootstrap theory of the time rate of exploitation of fossil fuel-bearing properties. Current expectations of producers about future prices relative to costs play the pivotal role. Accordingly, relative stability over time in prices and production of energy resources requires that most producers believe that tomorrow will not be significantly different from the recent past, although the market can perhaps accommodate some divergence of views among producers as long as producers expect stability on average.

Competition in such markets will provide intertemporal stability of prices and production flows only if the views of the competitors either coalesce in the belief that the future will not be significantly different from the recent past, or if the views of the competitors differ as to whether user costs are positive or negative in such a way that the "average" view is that user costs are zero. If, even with competition, most producers expect a significant change in prices relative to costs in the future, the current rate of exploitation will be accelerated (that is, if user costs are, on average, negative) or retarded (if average user costs are positive).

Thus, in the 1930s the discovery of the huge East Texas fields touched off expectations of large negative user costs (in other words, expectations of wellhead price declines) in an industry that at that time was relatively competitive—at least in the state of Texas at the wellhead stage. The result was a disastrously rapid rate of exploitation of domestic oil fields which brought about the fulfillment of the expectations of rapidly declining wellhead prices relative to costs. (The moral of this historical episode is that expectations of rapidly changing prices relative to costs in this industry can encourage behavior which will make the prophecy self-fulfilling, if the expectations are widely held and not readily altered.) State government-enforced market prorationing (proportional cutbacks in wellhead production), supported by the 1935 federal Connally Hot Oil Act, was required to alter these negative user cost expectations of competitive producers and stabilize the domestic industry. In later years, as foreign oil became important in world supplies, the operation of import quotas plus state market prorationing effectively eliminated any strong negative user cost expectations by domestic producers. At the same time, user cost speculation in the international market was restrained by the ability of the "Seven Sisters" to maintain an orderly market.

Most sellers of energy resources have, however, been led to expect rapidly rising prices by the events of the early seventies. The most important of these include the relaxation of prorationing arrangements in Texas and other oil-producing states, the growth of the power of the Organization of Petroleum Exporting Countries (OPEC) at the same time as import quotas were being removed, and the unsettled politics of the Middle East. These events have stimulated speculative proclivities and consequently retarded current production of fossil fuels and other energy sources such as uranium.

Current events have created an environment where most domestic energy producers and property owners expect rapidly rising wellhead prices of natural gas, old crude oil, and coal (as conglomerates "require" equal returns from each division). Even the price of "new" crude is expected to rise as OPEC turns the cartel screw a little tighter and tries to "catch up" to some extent with the world inflationary forces that the cartel released in the recent past, and politicians talk about removing all controls from wellhead prices or permitting U.S. prices to rise to world levels. Currently regulated wellhead prices in the United States are below what the market could be forced to pay (that is, demand is in the price inelastic range), while competitive fuels are controlled by growing monopolies, such as OPEC, and separate but not independent divisions of the same "energy companies." Congress, meanwhile, continues to hold public hearings to determine whether the wellhead price should be increased or even decontrolled. All these factors encourage producers to expect, at worst, no change in the existing price; and at best, a substantial increase. In other words, producer expectations are biased in the direction of price increases as monopolistic control of supply is validated by events and governmental policies—and hence speculative expectations can have a significant impact on diminishing current supply offerings. User cost considerations currently dominate discussions as to the rate at which energy resources should be exploited.

Keynes once pointed out (1936) that economic progress depends on the spirit of Enterprise, which in this context refers to the activity of producers motivated by a desire for action rather than inaction, and operating under reasonably stable conditions in an uncertain world, to produce a steady flow of output for the economy. Keynes recognized that in an uncertain world some men's proclivities would always influence them to try making speculative profits via supply manipulations, and he noted, "Speculators may do no harm as bubbles on a steady stream of Enterprise. But the position is serious when Enterprise becomes the bubble on a whirlpool of Speculation." The current critical supply situation for natural gas and oil in the United States, and the cartelized supply of all fossil fuels in the world, is in part due to Enterprise becoming engulfed in Speculative practices. Underlying the situation are the positive user costs expectations generated by the growing power of a worldwide energy cartel.

The evidence of monopoly restraint

What evidence is there that the current energy shortage is due to the fact that the monopoly constraint on supply leads to expectations of future further monopoly profits (user costs), rather than being due to increasing costs of production? During the years 1962 through 1972—when, until the very end of the period, prices were not rising— world consumption of petroleum increased by 107.4 percent, while world crude oil proved reserves increased by 108.5 percent (Davidson et al., 1974). In other words, the world was not facing any greater threat of running out of crude oil in 1972 than it was in 1962. Moreover, historically, the real price of oil had declined as reserves and production grew for the first hundred years of the oil industry. Yet suddenly, we were told that nature's supply of oil was dwindling rapidly and that only prices several hundred percent greater than those prevailing in the early seventies could increase supply substantially—and even that increment would be all but gone by the turn of the century (if Energy Secretary James Schlesinger was to be believed). Thus, the conventional view, as expressed by orthodox economist Schlesinger, was that the law of increasing production costs (and not an artificial cartel restriction) had finally caught up with the profligate consumer. Hence, the Carter-Schlesinger policy proposals for conservation of oil with higher prices (through taxes, so that the income goes mostly to the government rather than to the producers).

Studies carried out for the Brookings Institution and the Ford Foundation from a post-Keynesian perspective (Davidson et al., 1974, 1975) have attempted to estimate the elasticity of production costs for oil and gas, separating these costs from the "user costs" which could drive a significant wedge between supply price responses of oil producers to demand and their production costs. These studies indicate that if user costs could be eliminated by public policy, real production costs would have to rise only modestly to $7.00-$9.00 a barrel in 1978 dollars for the United States to achieve virtual independence from the OPEC cartel. To eliminate the user costs, however, the present exploitable market position of the energy cartel and its willing industry supplicants must either be weakened or eliminated.

The existence of an exploitable monopoly position depends on the present and future price elasticity of demand in the relevant price range. As far as the OPEC cartel is concerned, therefore, it depends in large measure on the current price in consuming countries and ultimately on the supply price at which alternative sources of energy will become significant substitutes for OPEC oil. Suppose, however, that the supplier of a substitute energy source also has an economic interest in OPEC petroleum reserves because it is a conglomerate energy company with an OPEC concession or has other large oil reserves. It must then take into account the positive user cost in providing any substitute fuels. This positive user cost will raise the supply price (above resource costs).

In these circumstances, the positive user cost of substitutes internalizes a cost that in a competitive economy would be external to the firm. Independent producers of domestic oil, shale, tar sands, coal, uranium, and so on (provided they were not permitted to share the monopoly returns of the major energy companies) would not care if they inflicted capital losses on the value of foreign underground reserves of petroleum by providing a cheaper energy source. The existence of rational, multisource, energy-producing conglomerates, however, constrains production of substitute fuels, makes monopolistic control of energy markets easier, and reduces consumer welfare. The ability of conglomerates to maintain high prices for substitute sources of energy tends to reinforce their monopoly power in marketing their OPEC oil.

If, at the current price, consumer demand for OPEC oil is therefore still in the exploitable range, a strong cartel of oil-producing nations can allow multinational energy conglomerates to continue to raise prices relative to real resource costs. The continuous revenue increases of host nations since 1970 seem to be attempts to search out the points at which demand for OPEC oil becomes so elastic that monopoly rents are fully exploited. (Higher prices require production restrictions, however, and hence the market-sharing arrangements that have been worked out to prevent one member of the cartel from increasing its gains at the expense of others.) Since the multinational energy companies also have vested interests in the price of OPEC reserves, they are willing to support the OPEC cartel by maintaining an "orderly" production market in all fossil fuels. Thus, monopolistic and speculative withholding reinforce each other and merge into one.

The policy implications

The policy implications of the foregoing analysis are easily drawn. Public policy must:

(1) Create an elastic demand for imported oil by encouraging the existence of many independent domestic producers of energy who cannot share in the monopoly rents of OPEC and the multinational energy conglomerates.

(2) Squelch producer speculation activities in all energy sources.

(3) Provide incentives for individual OPEC members to cheat on the cartel by removing the international energy companies as a mechanism for enforcing OPEC price decisions.

Speculation can be squelched in either of two ways:

A regulated wellhead price policy can be adopted, to create an atmosphere of certainty that any future price increases relative to production costs will be at an annual rate so small as to be below the annual interest charge on inventory. Once this has been done, it will never pay to speculate on inventories (for example, if ceiling prices never increase by more than the cost of borrowing short-term funds). The alternative is to create conditions which make expectations of a future price decline just as likely as an increase, so that individuals' speculative expectations tend to cancel. Bluntly, in the current context, this means permitting those who have withheld production in order to profit by it to be so well rewarded by the "free" market that it would appear to many that consumers no longer have any more wealth or income to be exploited.

Unfortunately, President Ford's energy policy (which would have led to a further shift of income and wealth from energy consumers to energy producers and royalty owners), President Carter's energy program (which only slightly modifies the income redistribution features of the Ford plan), and the OPEC strategy of regaining some of the extorted real income it lost due to the inflation of consuming countries' price levels, all point to the second means of squelching speculation. The problem with this approach is that it will inevitably exacerbate the inflationary and recessionary problems of the U.S. economy.

Conclusion

The current world energy crisis illustrates the importance of analyzing, as a post-Keynesian approach does, such factors as monopoly power and user costs in trying to understand the production flows and market prices of natural resources— especially when these flows and prices are changing rapidly and unexpectedly in the face of slowly expanding world output. Unlike the Pavlovian response of neoclassical equilibrium theorists, post-Keynesian analysts do not immediately see rising natural resource prices as evidence *per se* that the law of diminishing returns is operating in perfectly competitive markets—or, in other words, that we are running out of cheap energy and other raw materials. A post-Keynesian perspective would instead suggest that such price changes can best be understood (and an appropriate policy response formulated) by analyzing the behavior of entrepreneurial agents and resource property owners in terms of perceived market power and/or expectations about the future.

In this connection, Keynes' concept of "user cost" is a critical one. Keynes recognized that the "user cost" concept applied not only to raw materials such as fossil fuels, but to all capital equipment, "for in deciding his scale of production an entrepreneur has to exercise a choice between using up his equipment now and preserving it to be used later on." For Keynes, the concept of user costs was the keystone of his analysis of production; and in *The General Theory* he insisted, "*Supply price* is, I think, an incompletely defined term, if the problem of defining user costs has been ignored . . . . The exclusion of user cost from supply price . . . is inappropriate to the problem of supply price of a unit of output for an individual firm."

For those who adopt the post-Keynesian approach to economic analysis, the decision to utilize natural resources is therefore viewed as similar to that of disinvestment in capital equipment, while the search for new sources of natural resources is merely a form of capital investment. These positive and negative investment activities depend on the hopes, dreams, and fears of mortals—or what Keynes called "animal spirits." And thus there is a need to take seriously Keynes' admonition that "there is no clear evidence from experience that the investment policy which is socially advantageous coincides with that which is [thought to be] most profitable." Natural resource utilization, like all investment activities, will generate specific patterns of growth, employment, and income distribution. Economists, if they follow a post-Keynesian approach, should be able to indicate what will be the consequences of different patterns of natural resource use—just as they would for any change in gross and net investment activity. But at the same time they should be careful to indicate that the pattern which is discerned as socially desirable need not be that which, under given market conditions, appears to be most profitable to entrepreneurs.

ALFRED S. EICHNER

A Look Ahead

The United States and the world's other advanced countries with market economies seem to be caught in the grip of economic forces they cannot understand and therefore cannot master. Despite the best efforts of government, the dollar and other currencies continue to depreciate in value, certainly at home and in some cases even internationally. A resort to policies based on conventional theories in economics, whether those policies involve reduced public spending, curtailed growth of credit, or some combination of the two, has so far proved incapable of moderating the inflationary trend—except at the cost of increased unemployment and reduced economic growth. Indeed, during the most recent period, beginning in the early 1970s, recession and inflation have often gone hand in hand, giving rise to the trauma of "stagflation."

In light of the analysis presented in the preceding essays, it is hardly astonishing that public economic policy—what used to be termed political economy—should find itself in so sorry a state. For the policy, not only in the United States but throughout the North Atlantic and Pacific Oceanic community of market-oriented economies, is based on the neoclassical paradigm in economics, a paradigm that is both pre-Keynesian and pre-scientific. In other words, it involves

Alfred S. Eichner

the same conceptual framework, formulated to demonstrate the self-correcting nature of market mechanisms, that Keynes had to overcome in his day. Moreover, the theory initially obtained its hold on men's minds, and continues to retain that hold today, without having to meet the types of tests which are necessary to establish a paradigm in the natural sciences.

Those who are accustomed to thinking of the policies which governments have pursued since the end of World War II as "Keynesian" will be surprised by this statement. But that is only because they are confusing Keynesian theory with the "neoclassical synthesis"—developed by Paul Samuelson and his colleagues in Cambridge, Massachusetts—which has come to dominate the academic economics of the day. Under that synthesis, Keynes' argument (1936) that the economy may settle down at less than full employment is accepted, at least as a temporary result. In fact, since the time required for the economy to return on its own to a full employment level of output may prove longer than is politically tenable— in part because of the frictions in the market caused by trade unions and other types of monopolies—the government may be well advised to intervene through fiscal and monetary means to hasten the eventual return to full employment. But those concessions aside, the pre-Keynesian theory, with its emphasis on supply and demand determining price-and-quantity relationships under competitive conditions, is still regarded as an essentially correct analysis of the functioning of a modern, technologically advanced economy based on market institutions.

The preceding essays in this volume have shown how, in dealing with each of the major subtopics within economics— macrodynamics, pricing, income distribution, money, production, international trade, taxation, labor, and natural resources—the neoclassical theory falls short of providing a convincing explanation. In some cases, it is because the

166

assumptions underlying the theory are so at variance with what is known about the real world of economic institutions. In other cases, it is because the theory fails to account for certain types of historically observed phenomena. And in a few cases, it is because the logic of the theory itself is questionable. While the deficiencies in the orthodox approach may not be clearcut in the case of every one of the subtopics surveyed, the overall critique of neoclassical theory as a coherent explanation of how a modern, technologically advanced economy functions is a devastating one. The wonder is that scholars continue to propound it and that statesmen continue to accept advice based on it. Keynes well knew of what he spoke when he lamented (1936) the power that "some academic scribbler of a few years back" had been able to exercise over the minds of those who considered themselves to be men of practical affairs.

The purpose of this concluding essay, however, is not to sum up the case against neoclassical theory, nor even to explain why it continues to hold sway within the academic world. The latter would require a digression into the sociology of knowledge. The purpose rather is to suggest what may lie beyond the progress that post-Keynesian economists have already made in developing a comprehensive alternative to the neoclassical paradigm.

As several of the previous essays have pointed out, post-Keynesian theory is still in its formative stage. While the broad outlines of the new paradigm can already be discerned, much of the detailed argument remains to be worked out. What it offers is the prospect of uninhibited inquiry, and not the promise of quick and simple solutions to long vexing problems. Indeed, the theory's first important contribution will be to free economics as a discipline from the intellectual dead weight of neoclassical orthodoxy. This should be as invigorating to the cumulative growth of economic knowledge as the overthrow of the geocentric theory was to astronomy and the overthrow of the ether theory was to physics.

The gradual adoption of a post-Keynesian perspective is likely to revitalize economics, offering a theoretical framework which is more open-ended and therefore more conducive to productive inquiry, but it is not likely to bring immediate results or pat answers. This is because the post-Keynesian principles, if faithfully adhered to, will reveal that the problems which currently bedevil economics, both as a discipline and as a guide to public policy, are even less tractable than has been suspected. The advantage of the post-Keynesian approach is that it enables one to confront the problems directly and openly rather than to conceal them under simplifying assumptions. To elaborate on this point, it is necessary to delve more fully into the two areas—theory and policy—in which economics is presently stymied as a result of the neoclassical orthodoxy. Once the probable impact of the shift to a post-Keynesian perspective in each of these two areas has been described, together with the probable limitations on what can be achieved, the ground will have been laid for pointing out the intractability of the problems in yet a third area. That is the area of politics itself.

Necessarily, the views expressed here are personal. Post-Keynesian economists are so diverse in their outlook that it is hardly to be expected that they would all share these views. Still, this essay will serve to indicate what at least one member of the group sees as the most important implications, in terms of theory and policy, of the eventual displacement of the current neoclassical orthodoxy by the alternative post-Keynesian paradigm.

Substitution effects and income effects

As the neoclassical orthodoxy gradually gives way to a post-Keynesian approach, the nature of economics as an intellectual discipline is likely to change in three important ways. At the most obvious—though not necessarily the most fundamental—level, the emphasis is likely to shift from the analysis of substitution effects to the analysis of income effects. The Walrasian model which forms the core of neoclassical theory encompasses little more than substitution effects. Within the logic of the model, the demand for one good can increase only at the expense of the demand for another good, and then only because the relative price of the former has fallen. Similarly, one type of input, such as capital goods, can be used more intensively in the production process only at the expense of another type of input, such as labor, and then again only because the relative price of the former has fallen. This approach usually eliminates by assumption the possibility that the demand for all goods and the use of all types of inputs may increase together—at differing rates, to be sure—as a result of the higher income and level of demand which economic growth brings with it. Reliance on the neoclassical model makes it difficult, therefore, to provide a plausible and coherent explanation of economic growth.

In the more sophisticated versions of neoclassical theory, some income effects, it is true, are allowed for. But still, it is the substitution effects arising from a change in relative prices which provide the impetus for the shift from one static equilibrium position to another, and thus it is only the substitution effects which make any real difference in the models. In contrast, the economists responsible for developing the post-Keynesian alternative have found that, if a plausible and coherent explanation for such real-world phenomena as economic growth and cyclical fluctuations is to be provided, it is not enough simply to take into account the income effects, making them an integral part of the analysis. It is also necessary to recognize that the income effects generally swamp the substitution effects—if they do not eliminate them altogether.

Keynes (1936) was the first to point this out. It was he who called attention to the fact that a decline in wages, rather than encouraging the substitution of labor for capital equipment, would instead depress business confidence and business investment, thereby increasing the number of unemployed workers. But others, following in his path, have come to the same type of conclusion—namely, that whether the issue be long-period growth, short-period fluctuations, the distribution of income, the pattern of trade, or one of the other topics covered in this volume, it is the level and compotion of investment, together with the income effects which derive from that investment, which are the principal operative factors, not any change in relative prices. Econometric studies have led to the same type of conclusion, and it seems that only the dead weight of the neoclassical orthodoxy has prevented the economists who work inductively from generalizing this result into an empirical principle.

But the emphasis on income effects does have a disadvantage: It makes neat solutions difficult to obtain. Indeed the results are likely to be more open-ended. When the scope of the analysis is restricted to substitution effects, as it is in the neoclassical approach, there is always some new equilibrium position which a change in relative prices will bring about, and that new position can be determined simply by solving the set of mathematical equations that define the new system (or, in a partial analysis, by examining the point of intersection between the new supply and demand curves). When the income effects are fully allowed for, however, as they must be in a post-Keynesian approach, there need not be any new equilibrium position. Rather, the change in investment or whatever else has produced the income effects is likely to initiate a process (or, more accurately, modify a process already under way) without a determinable end state. In other words, the analysis shifts from logical time to historical time in which the future cannot be predicted because of the complex nature of the interaction among the different social subsystems that comprise the larger system. This points to a second change in the nature of economic analysis which the eventual acceptance of a post-Keynesian approach portends.

The systems approach

Economics as a social science is largely the outgrowth of the eighteenth-century mechanistic view of the universe which Newton's *Principia* inspired. It is based on the assumption that effects can be clearly distinguished from causes, and that the latter can explain the former. Despite the limitations of this philosophical framework when it comes to analyzing social and other biological phenomena, there was, until recently, little else to fall back on except Hegelian dialectics. Over the last several decades, however, quite a different philosophical framework has emerged, one that encompasses Newtonian mechanics and Hegelian dialectics as special cases. This is the systems, or cybernetic, approach. The advantage which it offers social scientists is that it can incorporate within its analytical structure (a) purposeful activity, (b) cumulative processes, and (c) the interaction of subsystems, both as part of a larger systems dynamic and in response to feedback from the environment. The systems approach is the most general approach available to social scientists, including economists.

Under the systems approach, economics is no longer the study of how scarce resources are allocated. It is instead the study of how an economic system—defined as the set of social institutions responsible for meeting the material needs of society's members—is able to expand its output over time by producing and distributing a social surplus. It is not just that the rate of expansion is likely to be uneven. It is also that the expansion has no discernible fixed limit, and that indeed the very process of expansion is likely to change the nature of the system in an unpredictable way. Although the

Alfred S. Eichner

final end state cannot be deduced—because the analysis is concerned with historical time—the process of expansion, that is, the dynamics of the system, can be intelligently analyzed.

When the economic system is seen as just one of several major societal systems, each with its own particular dynamics, the way is opened to a truly interdisciplinary attack on social problems. But even when the economy is viewed in isolation, the principles of systems theory still hold. This means that the interaction among the different component parts, for example, between business firms and households or between financial and nonfinancial sectors, must be analyzed in terms of input, output, and feedback. The last is especially important if the behavior of the system as a whole is to be understood.

From a post-Keynesian perspective, it is the behavior of the system as a whole, constituted as a set of historically specific institutions, which economic theory must be capable of explaining. This is the first step toward a better informed public policy. Once the system can be modeled to simulate the types of dynamic behavior actually observed in the real world—and this means cycles as well as long-run expansion, inflation as well as rising standards of living—the basis will be laid for more effective government intervention, whether this takes the form of manipulating the system as it presently exists or restructuring some essential component. This brings us to the third way in which economics is likely to change as a result of the post-Keynesian challenge.

The importance of empirical testing

The discipline of economics has so far successfully resisted all efforts to alter its character as an exercise in how to reason deductively from axiomatic principles. That is, it has insisted on remaining the Euclidian geometry of the social sciences.

This Cartesian position has not been without its advantage to economists themselves. They have been known to remark, "We travel with a light tool kit." By this, they mean that economic theorists have not had to burden themselves much with factual detail. They have been content to reason *a priori* —and hence their preference for elegance over relevance. But for economics as a discipline, this has meant falling short of being a modern science. What is missing is the same standard for judging the validity of a theory which prevails among natural scientists. This is the criterion that a theory must not just avoid logical error but that it also must account for the full range of empirically observable phenomena— which, in the social context, consist of the real world's historical events.

Some economists can be expected to take exception to this statement, pointing out, with some justification, that one of the most promising developments in the field over the past several decades is the growing insistence on empirical proof for any theoretical arguments that may be offered. Indeed, the work of post-Keynesian economists is often rejected on these very grounds. But this riposte ignores two points. The first is that the received, orthodox theory is usually exempted from any empirical test of its validity—especially if some mathematical, or formal, proof can be adduced. The second is that most of the empirical testing carried out so far has presumed the correctness of the orthodox theory; and while a large body of anomalous evidence has nonetheless emerged from these studies, as well as from other econometric investigations, the orthodox neoclassical theory has yet to be subjected to any rigorous empirical testing—in which its explanatory power could be directly compared with that of alternative formulations such as the post-Keynesian theory outlined in this volume.

The empirical testing of a theory is a tricky business, even more so in the social sciences than in biology or in the

natural sciences generally. Controlled experiments are out of
the question, and the historical data that the social scientist
must fall back on are subject to all sorts of measurement
error and other unknown influences. What this means is that
even the best constructed models provide only an imperfect
test of the theory they are meant to reflect. This is not an
argument against attempting to construct better models.
They do provide at least a first test of theories. It is rather to
make the point that a theory in the social sciences can be
accepted as valid only after, having been incorporated into
public policy, it produces the predicted results. It is on these
grounds that the Keynesian theory, as a guide to preventing
large-scale unemployment, must be deemed a success and the
neoclassical synthesis, as a guide to achieving full employment without inflation, must be judged a failure. Ultimately,
then, the test of the post-Keynesian theory outlined in the
essays in this volume will be whether it enables the United
States and the world's other advanced countries with market
economies to develop a more efficacious set of economic
policies, bringing the problems of inflation and trade deficits
under control without sacrificing economic growth and
employment. To pursue this point further, it is necessary to
shift the discussion from theory to policy.

Incomes policy

The preceding essays have been like a chorus in arguing that
inflation cannot be brought under control—except at too
great a cost in terms of reduced output and higher unemployment—unless the conventional policy instruments for regulating the economy are supplemented by an incomes policy.
One might reasonably conclude, therefore, that all a government need do to give its economic policies a post-Keynesian
orientation is to add an incomes policy to the existing stock
of intervention devices. Such a reading, however, greatly over-

simplifies what the post-Keynesian critics of orthodox theory have to say. It also fails to explain why governments have so far had little success in implementing incomes policies. The point is that what an incomes policy represents is not the starting point for a change in public policy, but rather the final move in an anti-inflationary effort requiring other, antecedent changes in public policy. In other words, post-Keynesian theory can point to the series of steps by which inflation and some of the world's other current economic maladies might eventually be brought under control, but it offers no "quick-fix" solutions.

Still, an incomes policy is the necessary capstone to an effective anti-inflationary program. However, this does not mean an incomes policy as that term is understood both by trade union critics and by some advocates. An incomes policy is not just a device for limiting the wage gains of organized workers. Rather, it represents a means of determining the annual, noninflationary rise in all the different types of income that accrue to households—dividends and rents as well as wages and salaries. And it reflects the post-Keynesian view of inflation as being the process by which prices rise to deflate nominal incomes, thereby bringing real incomes into line with the availability of real resources. While some would argue that the profits earned by business should be included within the scope of an incomes policy, this position ignores the distinction which post-Keynesian theory makes between the profits retained by the firm to finance invest-ment and the profits paid out to the owners as personal income. It is only the latter which an incomes policy need concern itself with.

Moreover, in a democratic society, an incomes policy of the sort just described cannot simply be imposed. It must instead gain acceptance among the different economic interest groups as the fairest and most equitable basis for distributing the fruits of technological progress which emerge in the form of higher output per worker. This means that a consensus must be reached, through the appropriate representative bodies, about the principles which will govern the apportionment of any social surplus. It also means facing up frankly and honestly to the distributional issues involved. Indeed, the reason the neoclassical synthesis has been of so little help in fashioning an effective anti-inflationary policy is that, by focusing on the "marginal productivity" of unmeasurable quantities like "capital," it misconstrues the nature of these distributional issues. Thus an incomes policy needs to be preceded, at the political level, by some minimal societal agreement as to how the gains from economic growth are to be distributed. The fact that the market alone is incapable of rendering this judgment is what makes an incomes policy essential.

Investment and growth

The distributional issues cannot be approached in isolation, however. As several preceding essays have pointed out, they are inextricably linked to investment and growth issues. Indeed, the latter form the core of political economy. Once the rate and composition of investment have been determined, the economy's dynamic growth path has been largely set. For the long-run rate of expansion, and with it the growth of output per worker, depends on the rate at which supply capacity—both business plant and equipment and social infrastructure—is being increased. And the short-period fluctuations around that trend line depend on how steadily the growth of investment and other forms of discretionary spending are being maintained. Moreover, it is a matter of quality as well as of quantity. Just any type of spending will not do—only the projects that will yield the highest marginal gains in supply capacity relative to the outlay, so that the secular rate of expansion is maximized. What must be recognized is that, contrary to the conventional neoclassical argument, the market cannot be fully relied upon to assure the bests results in this regard. And while the rate and especially the composition of investment are not easily regulated at the aggregate level through government policy, still, unless the representatives of key interest groups—trade unions, corporations, farmers, consumers, etc.—have some voice in these questions, they will be unable to serve their constituencies' interests in what matters to them most. The rate of inflation and the relative distribution of income among households, as determined by an incomes policy, are certainly important, but the growth of real income over time, as determined by the rate and composition of investment, is even more important.

Pricing

Distribution and investment are, however, only two of the three legs to the post-Keynesian triangle. The third involves the pricing mechanism. Orthodox theorists have led public policy badly astray by insisting that the only relevant issue is whether resources are being optimally allocated. But the pricing mechanism also plays a central role in providing investment funds for business and in determining relative income shares. The interrelationship among these three critical sets of factors is made more complex by the fact that in an advanced economy like that of the United States, there are two quite different types of markets, whose pricing and investment behavior vary from each other. There are the competitive markets, largely involving primary products, which are the focal point of orthodox theory, and the oligopolistic markets—dominated by large corporations and found primarily in the technologically more progressive sectors of the economy—about which the orthodox theory is mostly silent. In the former, prices are governed by supply and demand factors and investment is unplanned. In the latter, prices are cost-determined and planning, based on the long-term capital expansion programs of the individual corporate giants, is the rule. Thus there is no model, or set of policies based on a model, that applies across the board to both the competitive and oligopolistic markets. Indeed, in the competitive sector, the government must make up for the lack of inter-firm coordination and planning, while in the oligopolistic sector, it must make sure that the private power to plan does not subvert any larger public interest.

Once the interrelationship among distribution, investment, and pricing is properly understood, it becomes clear that fashioning an effective anti-inflationary policy is no easy task and that simply adopting an incomes policy will not suffice. The task is made even more difficult by the fact that each national economy, like that of the United States, is part of a larger world economic system—one that is little understood by economists of any stripe, post-Keynesian or otherwise. The instability of exchange rates, and the reverberating effects on domestic price and investment levels, point to this dimension of the world's current economic ills. Still, the task of fashioning an effective anti-inflationary policy is not a hopeless one, and if post-Keynesian theory offers no easy, quick solutions, it does at least point out the direction in which policy must move.

The criticism which it offers of the orthodox, neoclassical theory should, as a first step, seal off some of the blind alleys which public economic policy has entered. But, even more important than that, post-Keynesian theory suggests the sequence in which the set of essential, interrelated factors needs to be dealt with. Determining the rate and composition of investment is the first order of business. Only after those questions have been settled, thereby fixing the economy's dynamic growth path, can precise figures be attached to any pricing and incomes policies. Indeed, if the policies are based on a correct understanding of the role played by prices and relative income shares in the growth process, the derivation of the numbers should become a routine, almost technical matter. For if the post-Keynesian arguments are correct, it will be found that there is only one average profit margin and only one rate of growth of household income which, for the secular growth rate that has been chosen, will be noninflationary.

Public and private investment

It will, of course, be objected that determining the rate and composition of investment is beyond the power of government—at least without a radical transformation in the nature of the economic institutions found in developed countries like the United States. But this argument ignores the current reality. The fact is that at least a third of the total national income in developed countries like the United States already passes through the public sector. The real question is what use is to be made of those resources. Are they to be used, as investment in the infrastructure, to expand economic output? Are they to be used instead to achieve noneconomic ends? Or are they simply to be frittered away in boondoggles of one sort or another? Once the rate and composition of public investment have been determined in answer to these questions, then the rate and composition of private investment will largely fall into place. For, left to itself, private investment can be expected to adjust to the changing composition of final demand over which the government, through its own pattern of expenditures, exerts the predominant influence.

No, the more valid objection is that the government lacks the capacity to make better decisions about the rate and composition of public investment—not to mention the capacity to coordinate those expenditures with capital spending in the private sector as part of an overall, integrated plan. Thus it is not that the government lacks the means of imposing its blueprint on the economy. Rather it lacks the means of devising a workable blueprint—at least in the United States. In part, this is because false clues have been provided by orthodox theory, and these clues have led government to focus on the wrong issues. But it is also because the government has not properly structured itself to devise an overall blueprint. And this is a pity, since many of the requisite elements for a system of national indicative planning, to be carried out under government auspices, are already in place.

There is, first of all, the system of private planning based on the capital expansion programs of the nation's largest corporations. There is even an effort to coordinate these private plans through the forecasting and other services provided by groups such as the Conference Board, Data Resources, Inc., Chase Econometric Associates, and the Wharton Economic Forecasting Unit. Within government itself, there is an effort to bring coherence and foresight to spending within various areas—for example, transportation and energy, perhaps the two most critical areas insofar as the economic infrastructure is concerned. What is missing is some organ of government capable of fusing the results of these diverse efforts into a comprehensive plan, one that, because of its greater scope and coherence, would take precedence over other plans in guiding economic policy. Neither the Council of Economic Advisers and the Office of Management and Budget within the executive branch, nor the Congressional Budget Office, with the narrow political constituency they serve and the meager staff resources they command, can develop such a plan. It requires, instead, a new body—a planning secretariat functioning as the technical arm of a social and economic council on which would be represented, along with key public officials, all the private interest groups whose support is essential to the success of any incomes policy.

A new social contract

In this way—but only in this way—the basis would be laid for a "social contract" that would finally permit government to pursue a maximum growth or "full employment" policy without having to fear the inflationary consequences. In return for not exercising the market power which enables them to obtain higher than called-for increases in nominal income, thereby contributing to the wage-price inflationary spiral, the important interest groups— the nation's largest corporations and trade unions among them—would be given a more direct voice in determining the growth of real income. This would be the result of the influence which those interest groups were able to exert, through the social and economic council and its planning secretariat, on the rate and composition of public spending. Once that set of decisions had been reached, the rest—the rate and composition of private investment, the level of prices and the growth of real household income— would fall into place.

This is not to suggest that the working out of such a plan would be without its difficulties, both technical and adminis-trative. Nor would the creation of an effective planning mechanism at the national level solve all the world's current economic ills. But only along the lines suggested by post-Keynesian theory can an effective anti-inflationary policy be developed as the first step toward solving other types of problems. The post-Keynesian approach, by highlighting the role played by monetary institutions and uncertainty in the working of a market economy, as well as the role played by prices in redistributing income, also offers important insights into the nature of certain international economic problems. Still, from what has already been said, it should be clear that fashioning an effective anti-inflationary policy or dealing with other types of economic ills is not just a matter of theory or policy. It is also a matter of politics.

The politics of inflation

At one level, it would appear that putting the government in a position to cope more effectively with inflation requires only a slight enlargement of the considerable role which the government already plays in the economy—assuming, of course, that the dead weight of the orthodox, neoclassical theory were to be removed. To add an incomes policy to the existing arsenal of intervention devices, all that seems necessary is to superimpose a social and economic council, together with a planning secretariat, on the existing economic policy-making structure. This would involve only another incremental step in the long chain by which the existing structure has come into being—difficult as that next step might be to take in practice. But this assessment ignores perhaps the most fundamental point of the post-Keynesian explanation for inflation. And this is that inflation occurs because of conflicts over the relative distribution of income which are otherwise irreconcilable. (On closer examination, many of the international economic problems will, no doubt, be seen to involve the same types of conflicts.)

A social and economic council is merely a device for bringing those conflicts out into the open, providing a forum where, it is to be hoped, the genius of politicians can provide a temporary resolution so that the other business of the day can proceed. The result of the planning secretariat's analytical work should be to show that, for many of the issues posed, the nature of economic processes offers no real choice. Still, not all potential conflicts can be resolved solely on the basis of objective analysis. The rate of growth of output per worker governs only the average growth of real household income, not the relative distribution among households. Similarly, the secular rate of expansion governs only the average mark-up above costs, not the relative size of the mark-up among different industries. On a number of these and other finer details, considerable room for disputation will remain. An objective analysis, even with post-Keynesian theory serving as a guide, can only limit the range over which conflicts are likely to arise; it cannot eliminate the area of indeterminacy altogether. What this means is that, within whatever limits can be established on objective grounds, each of the interest groups represented on the social and economic council can be expected to push for a higher nominal income at the expense of other groups in society. Yet, if inflation is to be avoided, these competing claims must somehow be adjusted so that the total is held within the prescribed limits. This is precisely the type of issue which a democratic system of government has the greatest difficulty in resolving. Thus the effort to place a lid on inflation by relying on a social and economic council to come up with an acceptable incomes policy flies in the face of the wisdom reflected in both the Marxist and neoclassical alternatives to post-Keynesian theory.

The Marxist view is that a social and economic council would merely give legitimacy to the molding of economic policy on behalf of the more powerful economic interest groups in society. And indeed, under a democratic system of government, it is hard to see how it could be otherwise. The only question is whether those powerful economic interest groups need be entirely the same as those which now control the private system of economic planning already operating. The neoclassical theory, reflecting the nineteenth-century political philosophy upon which it is based, assumes that matters of relative income distribution, since they are so difficult for the political system to resolve, are best left to the market and other mechanisms. The mere fact that the market will handle a task badly is no reason to believe that the political system will produce any better result. Indeed, in taking on a task for which it is not suited, the political system may only undermine confidence in its efficacy and fairness.

What appears to be the only course that an effective anti-inflationary policy can take may therefore run aground either to port or to starboard. Only an optimist would argue that the policy could be steered clear either of being captured by an economically powerful elite, or of itself destroying the social cohesion that makes democratic government possible. In the pessimist's eyes, inflation may, in fact, be the least socially detrimental of the possible outcomes. If the government eschews the use of fiscal and monetary policies (which don't succeed in controlling inflation anyway), it will at least avoid the double penalty of stagflation. What better way to deal with what would otherwise be unmanageable social tensions over the relative distribution of income than to allow various economic interest groups, partly caught up in money illusion, to strike successive blows at the price level? As long as the inflation is kept within certain bounds, what harm is done?

Whether it is the optimist or the pessimist who sees the situation more clearly, there should at least be agreement that the achievement of an effective anti-inflationary policy— like the resolution of all other significant economic problems—is not just a matter of economic theory or even of policy. It is also a question of how mature the political institutions are. Have they finally developed to the point where they are able to handle the types of distributional issues which, up to now, would surely have damaged, if not entirely destroyed them? With regard to this last question—the political one—it is hard to be an optimist, at least for the near future.

Sources Cited

Ackoff, Russell L., and Fred E. Emery. *On Purposeful Systems*. Aldine 1972.

Adelman, M. A. *The World Petroleum Market*. Johns Hopkins University Press for Resources for the Future, 1972.

Asimakopulos, A., and John B. Burbidge. "The Short-Period Incidence of Taxation." *Economic Journal*, June 1974.

Asimakopulos, A. "A Kaleckian Theory of Income Distribution." *Canadian Journal of Economics*, August 1975.

Averitt, Robert T. *The Dual Economy:The Dynamics of American Industry Structure*. Norton, 1968.

Bain, Joe S. "Depression Pricing and the Depreciation Function." *Quarterly Journal of Economics*, August 1937.

————. *Barriers to New Competition*. Harvard University Press, 1956.

————. "A Note on Pricing in Monopoly and Oligopoly." *American Economic Review*, 1958.

Baumol, William. *Business Behavior, Value and Growth*. Harcourt, Brace & World, 1967.

Blaug, Mark. *Economic Theory in Retrospect*. Irwin, 1962.

Bowen, William G. *The Wage Price Issue: A Theoretical Analysis*. Princeton University Press, 1960.

Burbidge, John B. "Internally Inconsistent Mixtures of Micro- and Macrotheory in Empirical Studies of Profits Tax Incidence." *Finanzarchiv*, No. 2, 1976.

————. "Two-Sector Models of Inflation and Recession." McMaster

University Working Paper, No. 77-08.

Champernowne, D. G. "Expectations and the Links Between the Economic Present and Future." In *Keynes' General Theory: Reports of Three Decades*, edited by Robert Lekachman. St. Martin's Press, 1964.

Chick, Victoria. *The Theory of Monetary Policy*. Parkgate, 1977.

Cooper, Richard N. *International Finance: Selected Readings*. Penguin Books, 1974.

Cornwall, John. *Growth and Stability in a Mature Economy*. Wiley, 1972.

_____. *Modern Capitalism: Its Growth and Transformation*. St. Martins Press, 1978.

Cragg, J. G., Arnold C. Harberger, and Peter Mieszkowski. "Empirical Evidence of the Incidence of the Corporation Income Tax." *Journal of Political Economy*, December 1967.

Davidson, Paul. "Public Policy Problems of the Domestic Crude Oil Industry." *American Economic Review*, March 1963.

_____. "Inequality and the Double Bluff." In *Income Inequality. The Annals of the American Academy of Political and Social Science*, edited by Sidney Weintraub, September 1973.

_____, Laurence H. Falk, and Hoesung Lee. "Oil, Its Time Allocation, and Project Independence." *Brookings Papers on Economic Activity*, no. 2, 1974.

_____, Laurence H. Falk, and Hoesung Lee. "The Relations of Economic Rent and Price Incentives to Oil and Gas Supplies." In *Studies in Energy Tax Policy*, edited by G. M. Brannon, Ballinger Publishing, 1975.

_____. *Money and the Real World*. Macmillan, 2nd edition, 1978.

Davis, J. Ronnie. *The New Economics and the Old Economists*. Iowa State University Press, 1971.

Dell, Sidney. "Kalecki at the United Nations, 1946-54." *Oxford Bulletin of Economics and Statistics*, February 1977.

DeVroey, M. "The Transition from Classical to Neoclassical Economics: A Scientific Revolution." *Journal of Economic Issues*, September 1975.

Dobb, Maurice. *Theories of Value and Distribution Since Adam Smith*. Cambridge University Press, 1973.

Doeringer, P. B., and Michael Piore. *Internal Labor Markets and Manpower Analysis*. Lexington Books, 1971.

Domar, Evsey. *Essays in the Theory of Economic Growth*. Oxford University Press, 1957.

Eatwell, John. "On the Proposed Reform of Corporation Tax." *Bulletin of the Oxford Institute of Economics and Statistics*, November 1971.

Eichner, Alfred S., and J. A. Kregel. "An Essay on Post-Keynesian Theory: A New Paradigm in Economics." *Journal of Economic Literature*, December 1975.

Eichner, Alfred S. *The Megacorp and Oligopoly: Micro Foundations of Macro Dynamics*. Cambridge University Press, 1976.

_____, and Charles Brecher. *Controlling Social Expenditures: The Search For Output Measures*. Allenheld, Osmun, 1979.

Feiwel, George. *The Intellectual Capital of Michal Kalecki*. University of Tennessee, 1975.

Ferguson, Charles E. *The Neoclassical Theory of Production and Distribution*. Cambridge University Press, 1969.

Friedman, Milton. *The Optimum Quantity of Money and Other Essays*, Aldine, 1969.

Gaffney, M. Mason. "Soil Depletion and Land Rent." *Natural Resources Journal*, January 1965.

Galbraith, John Kenneth. *Money: Whence It Came, Where It Went*. Houghton Mifflin Company, 1975.

Garegnani, Pierangelo. *Il Capitale Nelle Teorie Della Distribuzione*. Giuffré, Milano, 1960.

_____. "Switching of Techniques." *Quarterly Journal of Economics*, November 1966.

_____. "Heterogeneous Capital, the Production Function and the Theory of Distribution." *Review of Economic Studies*, July 1970.

Ginzberg, Eli. *The Human Economy, A Theory of Manpower Development and Utilization*. McGraw-Hill, 1976.

_____. "The Job Problem." *Scientific American*, January 1977.

Godley, W. A. H., and W. D. Nordhaus. "Pricing in the Trade Cycle." *Economic Journal*, September 1972.

Gordon, David M. *Economic Theories of Poverty and Underemployment*. D. C. Heath, 1972.

Hall, Robert L., and C. J. Hitch, "Price Theory and Business Behaviour." *Oxford Economic Papers*, No. 2, 1939, reprinted in Wilson and Andrews, 1951.

Harberger, Arnold C. "The Incidence of the Corporation Income Tax." *Journal of Political Economy*, June 1962.

Harcourt, G. C., and Peter Kenyon. "Pricing and the Investment Decision." *Kyklos*, September 1976.

Harcourt, G. C. *Some Cambridge Controversies in the Theory of Capital*. Cambridge University Press, 1972.

_____. "The Theoretical and Social Significance of the Cambridge Controversy in the Theory of Capital: An Evaluation." *Revue D'Economie Politique*, March 1977.

Harrison, Bennet. "Institutions on the Periphery." In *Problems in Political Economy: An Urban Perspective*, edited by David M. Gordon. D. C. Heath, second edition, 1977.

Harrod, Roy F. "An Essay in Dynamic Theory." *Economic Journal*, March 1939.

_____. *Towards a Dynamic Economics*. Macmillan (London), 1948.

_____. *Economic Essays*. Harcourt, Brace, 1952.

Hartshorn, J. E. *Politics and World Oil Economics, An Account of the International Oil Industry in its Political Environment*, Praeger, 1967.

Hicks, John. "Mr. Keynes and the 'Classics': A Suggested Interpretation." *Econometrica*, April 1937.

_____. *Capital and Growth*. Oxford University Press, 1965.

_____. *The Crisis in Keynesian Economics*. Basil Blackwell, 1974.

_____. "What Is Wrong With Monetarism." *Lloyd's Bank Review*, October 1975.

Hines, Al. *On the Reappraisal of Keynesian Economics*. Humanities Press, 1971.

Jaffé, William. "The Normative Bias of the Walrasian Model: Walras Versus Gossen." *Quarterly Journal of Economics*, August 1977.

Johnson, Harry G. *International Trade and Economic Growth, Studies in Pure Theory*. Harvard University Press, 1958.

_____. *Money, Trade and Growth*. Allen and Unwin, 1962.

Kahn, R. F. *Selected Essays in Employment and Growth*. Cambridge University Press, 1972.

Kaldor, Nicholas. "Alternative Theories of Distribution." *Review of Economic Studies*, no. 2, 1956. Reprinted in Kaldor, 1960.

_____. *Essays on Value and Distribution*. Free Press, 1960.

_____. "Inflation and Recession in the World Economy." *Economic Journal*, December 1976.

Kalecki, Michal. *Studies in Economic Dynamics*. Allen and Unwin, 1943.

_____. *Theory of Economic Dynamics, An Essay on Cyclical and Long-Run Changes in Capitalist Economy*. Rinehart, 1954.

_____. *Studies in the Theory of Business Cycles, 1933-39*. Augustus Kelley, 1966.

_____. *Selected Essays on the Dynamics of the Capitalist Economy, 1933-70*. Cambridge University Press, 1971.

_____. *Essays on Developing Economies*. Humanities Press, 1976.

Keynes, John Maynard. *The Economic Consequences of the Peace*. Macmillan (London), 1920.

_____. *A Treatise on Money*. Macmillan (London), 1930. 2 vols.

_____. *The General Theory of Employment, Interest and Money*. Macmillan (London), 1936.

_____. *The Collected Writings of John Maynard Keynes*. Macmillan (London), 1973, Vols. VII, XIII, XIV.

Kregel, J. A. *Rate of Profit, Distribution and Growth: Two Views*. Aldine, 1971.

_____. *The Reconstruction of Political Economy: An Introduction to Post-Keynesian Economics*. Wiley, 1973.

_____. *The Theory of Capital*. Macmillan (London), 1976.

Kuller, Robert G., and Ronald G. Cummings. "An Economic Model of Production and Investment for Petroleum Reservoirs." *American Economic Review*, March 1964.

Kzyzaniak, M., and R. A. Musgrave. *The Shifting of the Corporation Income Tax*. Johns Hopkins University Press, 1963.

Lange, Oskar. *Introduction to Economic Cybernetics*. Pergamon Press, 1970.

Laszlo, Ervin. *Introduction to Systems Philosophy: Toward a New Paradigm of Contemporary Thought*. Gordon and Branch, 1972.

Leijonhufvud, Axel. *On Keynesian Economics and the Economics of Keynes*. Oxford University Press, 1968.

Lowe, Adolph. *The Path to Economic Growth*. Cambridge University Press, 1976.

_____. *On Economic Knowledge*. Enlarged edition. M. E. Sharpe, 1977.

McNulty, P. J. "Economic Theory and the Meaning of Competition." *Quarterly Journal of Economics*, December 1968.

Malthus, Thomas R. *Principles of Political Economy,*. 1820.

Marshall, Alfred. *Principles of Economics*. Macmillan (England), 1890 [8th ed., 1920].

Marx, Karl. *Capital*. International Publishers, 1967.

Meade, James E. *A Geometry of International Trade*. Allen and Unwin, 1952.

_____. *The Theory of International Economic Policy*. Oxford University Press, 1955.

Means, Gardiner C., ed. *The Roots of Inflation*. Burt Franklin, 1975.

Mieszkowski, Peter. "Tax Incidence Theory: The Effects of Taxes on the Distribution of Income." *Journal of Economic Literature*, December 1969.

Minsky, Hyman. *John Maynard Keynes*. Columbia University Press, 1975.

Moore, Basil. *An Introduction to the Theory of Finance*. Free Press, 1968.

Nell, E. J. "The Fall of the House of Efficiency." In *Income Inequality. The Annals of the American Academy of Political and Social Science*, edited by Sidney Weintraub, September 1973.

Pasinetti, Luigi. *Growth and Income Distribution*. Cambridge University Press, 1974.

_____. *Lectures on the Theory of Production*. Columbia University Press, 1977.

Reich, M., D. Gordon, and R. Edwards. "A Theory of Labor Market Segmentation." *American Economic Review*, May 1973.

Ricardo, David. "Principles of Political Economy (with Sraffa's Introduction)." *Works and Correspondence*, Vol. I, Cambridge University Press, 1951.

Robinson, Joan. "The Production Function and the Theory of Capital." *Review of Economic Studies*, no. 2, 1953.

_____. *The Accumulation of Capital*. Macmillan (London), 1956.

_____. *Essays in the Theory of Economic Growth*. Macmillan (London), 1962.

_____. *Economic Heresies.* Basic Books, 1971.

_____. "The Need for a Reconsideration of the Theory of International Trade." In *Collected Economic Papers*, Vol. IV, Blackwell, 1973.

Roncaglia, Alessandro. *Sraffa and the Theory of Prices.* Wiley, 1978.

Samuelson, Paul A. *Economics.* McGraw-Hill, 1948 [10th ed., 1976].

Schumpeter, Joseph. *History of Economic Analysis.* Oxford University Press, 1954.

Scitovsky, Tibor. "A Reconsideration of the Theory of Tariffs." *Review of Economic Studies*, no. 2, 1942.

Scott, Anthony D. "Notes on User Cost." *Economic Journal*, June 1953.

Shapiro, Nina. "The Revolutionary Character of Post-Keynesian Economics." *Journal of Economic Issues*, September 1977.

Shubik, M. "A Curmudgeon's Guide to Microeconomics." *Journal of Economic Literature*, June 1970.

Smith, Adam. *An Enquiry into the Nature and Causes of the Wealth of Nations*, edited by E. Cannon. Methuen & Co., 1904 (first edition, 1776).

Solow, Robert M. "The Economics of Resources or the Resources of Economics." *American Economic Review*, May 1974.

Sraffa, Piero. "Sulle Relazioni fra Costo e Quantita Prodotta." *Anni di Economia*, 1925.

_____. *Production of Commodities by Means of Commodities.* Cambridge University Press, 1960.

Sylos-Labini, Paolo. *Oligopoly and Technical Progress.* Harvard University Press, 1962.

Thurow, Lester C. *Generating Inequality.* Basic Books, 1975.

Tinbergen, Jan. *On the Theory of Economic Policy.* North-Holland, 1952.

Veblen, Thorstein. "Why Is Economics Not An Evolutionary Science?" In *The Place of Science in Modern Civilization*. B. W. Heubsch, 1919.

von Böhm-Bawerk, Eugen. *Capital and Interest.* Kelley, 1970.

Walras, Léon. *Elements d'Économie Politique Pure.* Allen and Unwin, 1954 (first published in French in 1874-1877).

Weintraub, Sidney. *Price Theory.* Pitman, 1949.

_____. "A Macroeconomic Approach to the Theory of Wages."

Sources Cited

American Economic Review, December 1956.

_____. *A General Theory of the Price Level, Output, Income Distribution and Economic Growth*. Chilton, 1959.

_____. "Keynes and the Monetarists." *Canadian Journal of Economics*, February 1971.

_____. *Capitalism's Inflation and Unemployment Crisis*. Addison-Wesley, 1978.

Wicksell, Knut. *Lectures on Political Economy*. 2 vols. ed. by Lionel Robbins, George Routledge and Sons, 1934, (first published in Swedish in 1901).

_____. *Value, Capital and Rent*. Allen and Unwin, 1954 (first published in German in 1893).

Wicksteed, P. "The Scope and Method of Political Economy in the Light of the 'Marginal' Theory of Value and Distribution." *Economic Journal*, March 1914.

Wilson, T., and P. W. S. Andrews. *Oxford Studies in the Price Mechanism*. Clarendon Press, 1951.

Wood, A. *A Theory of Profits*. Cambridge University Press, 1975.

Index

About the Authors

Eileen Appelbaum is Assistant Professor of Economics at Temple University. Her published work includes a chapter on "Radical Economics" in *Modern Economic Growth*, edited by Sidney Weintraub. She is currently doing research on the reentry of mature women into the labor force and on the vocational aspirations of high school students.

A. Asimakopulos is Professor of Economics at McGill University in Canada. He is the author of the textbook *An Introduction to Economic Theory: Microeconomics*. The articles he has published in scholarly journals include "A Kaleckian Theory of Income Distribution" in the May 1975 issue of the *Canadian Journal of Economics* and "The Short-Period Incidence of Taxation" (with John Burbidge) in the June 1974 issue of the *Economic Journal*.

John B. Burbidge is Assistant Professor of Economics at McMaster University in Canada. He is the author of "Internally Inconsistent Mixtures of Micro- and Macrotheory in Empirical Studies of Profits Tax Incidence" in *Finanzarchiv* (no. 2, 1976) and the co-author of "The Short-Period Incidence of Taxation" in the June 1974 issue of the *Economic Journal*.

Richard Chase is Professor of Economics at the University of Vermont. He has published several articles on Keynes in scholarly journals and is currently doing research on the nature of socioeconomic change, with particular emphasis on paradigmatic shifts.

John Cornwall is Professor of Economics, Dalhousie University, Canada. His published works include *Growth and Stability in a Mature Economy* and *Modern Capitalism: Its Growth and Transformation*. He is currently completing a study of stagflation.

Paul Davidson is Professor of Economics at Rutgers University and co-editor of the *Journal of Post Keynesian Economics*. He was formerly an assistant research director for the Continental Oil Company. His book *Money and the Real World* is one of the key works in the post-Keynesian literature on money and he has co-authored studies on the energy problem for both the Ford Foundation and the Brookings Institution.

Alfred S. Eichner is Professor of Economics at the State University of New York, College at Purchase, and Director, Center for Economic and Anthropogenic Research. He is the author of *The Emergence of Oligopoly: Sugar Refining as a Case Study* and *The Megacorp and Oligopoly: Micro Foundations of Macro Dynamics* and the co-author of *Controlling Social Expenditures: The Search for Output Measures*.

Peter Kenyon was, until he took up residence at the University of Virginia in 1977, a tutor at the University of Adelaide, Australia. He is the co-author, with Geoffrey Harcourt, of the article "Pricing and the Investment Decision," in the September 1976 issue of *Kyklos*.

About the Authors

J. A. Kregel is Professor of Economics at Livingston College, Rutgers University. He is the author of *Rate of Profit, Distribution and Growth: Two Views* and *The Reconstruction of Political Economy: An Introduction to Post-Keynesian Economics*.

Basil J. Moore is Professor of Economics at Wesleyan University in Connecticut. He is the author of two textbooks, *An Introduction to the Theory of Finance* and *An Introduction to Modern Economic Theory*. Among the articles he has published in scholarly journals is "The Endogenous Money Supply," which appeared in the September 1979 issue of the *Journal of Post Keynesian Economics*.

Alessandro Roncaglia is Professor of Political Economy at Perugia University in Italy. He is the author of *Sraffa and the Theory of Prices* and has contributed articles on the theory of value and distribution to both Italian and British journals.

3459